G Fernandz

WHO LIES HERE?

A New Inquiry into Napoleon's Last Years

The Bettman Archive

Napoleon on his death bed, St. Helena, 1821.
After contemporary drawing.

WHO LIES HERE?

A New Inquiry into Napoleon's Last Years

By THOMAS G. WHEELER

G. P. Putnam's Sons
New York

Copyright © 1974 by Thomas G. Wheeler

All rights reserved. This book, or parts thereof, must not be reproduced in any form without permission. Published simultaneously in Canada by Longman Canada Limited, Toronto.

SBN: 399-11321-5

Library of Congress Catalog
Card Number: 73-93750

PRINTED IN THE UNITED STATES OF AMERICA

The story of Napoleon produces a similar impression to that created by the Revelation of St. John: we all know there must be something more there, but we don't know what.

—Goethe

Contents

	PROLOGUE	1
Part One:	THE FURY FADES	15
Part Two:	EXITS AND AN ENTRANCE	69
Part Three:	TOKENS AND TESTAMENTS	131
	EPILOGUE	197

Prologue

Napoleon? Ah, that was the most beautiful countenance from which Genius ever looked upon Mankind!
—Winston Churchill

A GOOD many years ago a bright, birdlike and extremely knowledgeable Englishwoman formally introduced me to the baffling difficulties inherent in researching the Napoleonic literature. We fell into casual conversation outside the reading room of the British Museum, and soon she was initiating me in a rapid-fire series of terse, truncated sentences as we stood damply together under her tiny umbrella, waving vainly at the taxis as they rolled grandly and indifferently past us.

Most of my day, as I explained to her, had been squandered in discovering that optimistic methods of approach didn't work for the Emperor: It appeared there was altogether too much material available and quite obviously too few years in which to explore it—no matter what one's age. I was frustrated and a bit sullen, but soon my companion was in full spate, pouring out her distilled wisdom before me with generous vigor in spite of my glumness and the melancholy rain. I began paying closer attention, learning of many odd things.

"In two thousand years there's only these three men," she went on in her disjointed way. "These three, right up at the head of the procession . . . all the others trooping along miles in the rear —book-wise, that is. Dread getting a research job on any one of them . . . a week to get through the catalogue alone—that's on one

WHO LIES HERE?

only, mind you . . . but they're never up to date—can't be, you know, impossible . . . rivers of new titles every day, diaries unearthed, old records dug out . . . all over the world. And *you* had to start on one of *them!*"

She smiled bitterly, glancing up at me slantwise from beady eyes, and continued without a break into snatches of professional reminiscences, so that I was prevented from making the obvious request as to the identity of the forbidding three. There was too much expertise to be had here for the taking for me to interrupt rashly, and I waited for her to run down temporarily, and then slipped in my question.

"Napoleon, Shakespeare, and Jesus of Nazareth!" she replied promptly. "In that order . . . last shall be first or something. But by now I've stopped believing in 'em. Probably all fables—they're all too pat, too obviously manufactured, don't you see; set pieces, like Greek myths or stylized plays . . . your man's case the worst of the lot! Whoever made *him* up wrote a lot of silly mistakes . . . no twelves, for instance—zodiac, champions, disciples . . . should have stopped at twelve marshals instead of—what? Twenty-six? No artistic unity—*Hoy, taxi!*"

The staggering power of the hail emerging from so tiny a body not only astounded me but appeared to have stunned the driver into stopping, in spite of his sullen determination to go on. In a moment it was all over and they were gone into the drizzle—the little umbrella, too.

London seemed duller, and damper yet.

Napoleon Bonaparte, William Shakespeare, and Jesus the Christ: Probably no one really understands why these three personages, at the extreme apex of the world's recorded great (if their respective literatures be any criterion), have received and continue to command the unflagging interest of literate men. Just these three, seemingly so disparate, and even, perhaps, so out of order of

PROLOGUE

precedence. Many years later an irreverent Parisienne at the Bibliothèque Nationale commented, referring to Napoleon's outstanding position in the trio, *"Mais, que fait-il dans cette galère?"* ["But what's *he* doing in *that* company?"]

Possibly because, in an unconsciously conceived analogue of the human triad—body, mind and soul—it is necessary that some grand figure be cast for the first role; the other choices are inevitable. People have, at any rate, made the selection for themselves, with little concern for or deference to the moralists, the pedagogues or the dogmatists. The common factor in the choices is that each of the three was indisputably a genius of the first rank, the greatest in his genre for the Western world.

My English researcher was right, too, in her opinion about the stylized nature of their legends; their stories possess, in addition to the quality of truth, the earmarks of having been formulated by some master craftsman in command of cosmic professional resources as well as the arresting techniques of a sophisticated playwright. The latter at least was quite evidently on the job in the year 1769, when Napoleon Bonaparte was born into an impoverished middle-class family of Ajaccio, in the island of Corsica.

Of that year no prodigies are recorded, no chanting of ancestral voices or looming of celestial phantoms: None of those dire portents that in antiquity so often told of the coming of the earth shakers. Instead, it seems to have been a year of quiet preparation, as though our hypothetical playwright had been unobtrusively planting, all about the face of Europe, the projected *dramatis personae* of an epochal production, with rehearsals planned for a couple of decades ahead. Then would come the grand spectacle itself, unfolding to men's startled gaze with all the world for a stage.

First to arrive in that extraordinary year was he who would become the mighty Ney—the one Napoleonic marshal of whom

WHO LIES HERE?

everyone has heard, he whom his master named Bravest of the Brave, Prince of the Moskova, Duke of Elchingen. Indomitably supporting his chief through the scores of great battles, at the end his tragic death was decreed by his own countrymen. He was born in January.

For men of such caliber February was too short a month, it received no candidate, but in March came the natal day of the famous Marshal Soult: loyal and supremely competent. He outlived all the rest of the imperial cast, and was an honored guest at Queen Victoria's coronation, where the British made him his own ducal carriage for the parade.

In April came the *beau sabreur* and inspired leader of men, the intrepid Marshal Lannes: youngest of all the marshals and the first of them to die. It was to him that the poet Browning referred in his "Incident of the French Camp." There has rarely been a more romantic figure.

Then, with the advent of May, it appeared high time that the opposition put in an appearance: This month was assigned to the future Duke of Wellington, conqueror of so many of the marshals in Spain and finally, at Waterloo, of Napoleon himself.

To direct the Duke in his turn and thus, ultimately, all the others, June supplied a future Minister of England: Lord Castlereagh. From first to last he was to be the implacable foe of Bonapartism, the one man responsible for Britain's unrelenting will to crush Republicanism in France, he who at last decreed the exile of the humbled Emperor to St. Helena and all the unnecessary harshness of that imprisonment.

July was the month given over to Sir Hudson Lowe, a vindictive and petty man sent by Castlereagh to be the Governor of St. Helena: the jailor and tormenter of his contemptuously aloof charge—whom he delighted in referring to as "General Bonaparte."

PROLOGUE

That made three parts so far assigned to each side. Now that these future principals and chieftains were in position and safely launched, the time was indicated for the birth of the great figure who would set all these into purposeful motion, animating them, friend and foe alike, by the force of his will and genius. Accordingly therefore Napoleon Bonaparte first saw light in the month of August, on his Mediterranean island, from which on fair days he would be able to make out the tiny form of nearby Elba—another island he would come to know quite well.

(Those with astrological inclinations may be intrigued to note that both Hudson Lowe and Napoleon were born under the same zodiacal sign: Never, one may be reasonably sure, had two men differed more greatly!)

Napoleon, contrary to popular belief, began his career as a royalist officer, King Louis XVI having granted him a scholarship to the military academy at Brienne. It was the revolution, of course, that offered his great opportunity: He promptly changed sides, proceeding by sheer will, opportunism and innate military ability to fight his way to the vacant throne of France. Not to reign as a mere king, however, but as Emperor and as King of Italy as well, with an Austrian Archduchess as his Empress. This alliance had one quite curious result at the least—Napoleon could and did thereafter refer to the guillotined Louis, his predecessor, as "my uncle"!

After nearly twenty years of almost continuous warmaking, his increasingly ruthless career was halted by a last, successful coalition of the European powers. These huge armies were financed almost entirely by England, whose fleets dominated the world's seas and strangled the trade of the imperial ports by their blockade; additionally, Wellington drove right across Spain and through the Pyrenees, forcing large French armies ahead of him. Simultaneous

WHO LIES HERE?

with his entry into southern France came the occupation of Paris by the coalition forces, and Napoleon, virtually deserted by his army leaders, signed an act of surrender from the castle of Fontainebleau.

Considering the disasters and humiliations these European monarchs had suffered at his hands, the terms they dictated to the fallen Emperor in this Peace of Fontainebleau appear extraordinarily moderate. They agreed, with England's consent, to give him the small islet of Elba as a sort of token kingdom, and he was permitted to retain the title of Emperor. France engaged to give him an annual subsidy of two million francs, and he could take with him a personal military escort of four hundred men of his Old Guard, to be paid for from his own pocket. It was implied that his son, the King of Rome (now fled back to Austria), and the Empress Marie Louise would be restored to him.

Nowhere in the document is Napoleon described as a prisoner—yet, of course, this status was implicit. This delicacy and the leniency of the terms were in great part due to the influence and kindly pressures of the Czar Alexander, who had never entirely overcome an earlier infatuation with his one-time conqueror, in spite of the invasion of 1812 and other breaches of trust. The Russian Emperor was now the most influential and potentially powerful among the European powers, and his championing of Napoleon's interests without doubt saved the latter from a much more rigorous confinement. When his place of detention was being discussed his ex-Minister Talleyrand, arch-intriguer and conniver, urged that St. Helena be selected as more remote, isolated and readily guarded: a place of exile safer and more fitting. It was Alexander who overruled him and insisted that Elba was adequate. But that early, nevertheless, the name of the grim fortress-island was projected onto the skies of Napoleon's unpromising future, and into his awareness.

PROLOGUE

Some historian has noted that of all the signatories to the Peace of Fontainebleau, the only one to observe any of its terms was Napoleon: all the other blue-blooded subscribers perjured themselves from the start. The French, even under the Czar's and Wellington's prodding, paid not a cent for the exile's support, not a single franc of the two million they had promised. The Empress and the little King of Rome remained virtual prisoners in Vienna, both receiving intensive brain washing to cure them of any lingering attachment to the Emperor, and Marie Louise herself was systematically debauched, at her father's arrangement, by a dashing hussar officer who sired several illegitimate children in this quarter by "royal permission," so to speak.

The idea seems to have been that Napoleon, a "plebian upstart," "the Corsican adventurer" and all the similar weary terms showered on him for two decades by Europe's newspapers and handbills, was to be humiliated intolerably now that he was helpless and at their mercy—degraded and shown exactly what happened to parvenus, those who insolently intruded themselves among their betters. As for the terms of the Peace of Fontainebleau—do gentlemen bother about such things when they deal with the lower orders?

There was nothing for Napoleon to do, when he at last saw his real circumstances (and talk of St. Helena was again reported from the Council of Vienna, where the kings and their ministers had congregated to settle the frontiers of disrupted Europe). He could only escape and once more try his fortunes in France. The time was propitious, for the Bourbons once again were alienating everyone, having "learned nothing and forgotten nothing." To ship himself and his small force aboard the few vessels of his little "navy" and to disembark on the southern French coast was readily effected by one whose career had been spent in far more involved maneuvers with men and horses; the real mystery is how he managed to evade the

WHO LIES HERE?

British patrol vessels plying the waters between Elba and France. Many, at the time, were convinced that there had been collusion.

But the play was almost finished, nevertheless, the curtain beginning to tremble before its descent. Received by the French with acclamation, he was at once repudiated by the monarchs still, unfortunately for him, assembled in the Congress of Vienna and therefore able to take instant action. He was declared outlaw, and war against him commenced at once—with a unanimity rare among these jealous and rancorous sovereigns. Roughly three months after their declaration of war, Napoleon went out to meet a coalition of Prussian and British forces based in Belgium. After defeating the former at Ligny and separating the two armies, the latter held him in bloody combat at the little village of Waterloo until, in the evening, Blucher's Prussians were able to come up and rout the terribly mauled French. For the first time Napoleon saw an army led by him flee the field, hopelessly demoralized and helplessly butchered, while he too was compelled to ride in something approaching panic to escape the fury of a sort of warfare that had somehow gotten free of his practiced control.

It was the end, finally, of the great dream. Other generals had learned and even surpassed his techniques; France, weary of bloodshed, no longer permitted herself to be swayed by the thunderous oratory, the captured banners, the glorious uniforms and the panoply. The magic was all bled away.

Only a few days after the Waterloo disaster Napoleon had become a superfluity, even an embarrassment, to a government preparing to cope yet again with foreign invaders and willing to placate them with almost any sacrifice. Quite bluntly they let him see that he was no longer wanted, that there no longer existed any niche for such an anachronism. He appeared to have understood.

Finding that escape by sea had been rendered impossible by the presence of a British battleship at Rochefort, he brought himself at

PROLOGUE

last to the point of surrendering to the ship's captain and entrusting his fate to the British government. In daily consultation with the European kings and ministers now in Paris, Lord Castlereagh decided that St. Helena was the only place to which Napoleon could now be entrusted. All the time that elapsed while his fate was being determined Napoleon spent in Plymouth harbor on the *Bellerophon*—a grim reminder of Trafalgar and many a fierce sea battle before and after that. He *could* have been turned over to Louis XVIII, once more back on his throne, and there is no question of his fate had this economical course been adopted: He would instantly have been stood against a wall and shot. It would have saved the British taxpayer several million pounds and much anxiety in the coming years.

With Napoleon at last disposed of, the rulers and oligarchs heaved a mighty sigh of collective relief and prepared themselves with relish to settle comfortably back into the grand old feudal pattern, to resume the enjoyment of the so rudely interrupted privileges and perquisites of their birthright. Alas for them and their hopes—it was never to be the same again! The vanished Emperor had succeeded—perhaps in spite of himself, perhaps purposefully—in making a casual mockery of the concept of hereditary rulers, of Emperors and Kings by the Grace of God; he had created or unthroned so many at his whim, had made of himself one greater than any other: The odor of their sanctity was all but completely dissipated. As Cervantes had killed off, with the mockery of his pen, the persistent fantasy of medieval chivalry and its spurious enchantments, so had the implicit ridicule of Napoleon's arbitrary king-making destroyed forever the myth of divine right.

Perhaps—who can tell?—that was why the great drama was staged, what it was intended to effect: that it should by force of arms and ridicule sweep away moribund institutions otherwise

WHO LIES HERE?

capable of indefinite persistence because of men's greed and blindness and inertia; that it should admit the winds of the new century and its liberating and fructifying adumbrations—steam and electricity, representative government, universal education; that the true emancipation of man and woman might get under way. All that glorious promise had been waiting, impatiently, in the wings: high time to clear the stage, once again. But in this light Napoleon ought not to be—as he has been—thoughtlessly charged with impeding the "march of civilization." (He may have overstayed his time on the stage a little, according to the script; but it is hard to give up the limelight and the leading role and the applause! In this respect he was no worse than many another of history's bit players.) Rather, he should be seen as the select agent—none other was there to serve—of god or evolution or providence or whatever one chooses to name that ultimate destiny that is shaping our ends and whose purposeful promptings may be discerned at every significant period of our global history.

All this happened such a very short time ago, in terms of a man's lifetime: just the other day, so to speak. Consider these two illustrations.

Early in this century, and only a few years before I was born, there yet lived a Napoleonic officer named Lieutenant Markiewicz. He was a Pole, born in Cracow in 1794, and had enlisted in the Polish Lancers of the Imperial Guard while still a youngster. After many battles he had ridden to Moscow with the Emperor and the *Grande Armée* and ridden back, too, on that frightful retreat: the most appalling military disaster in all history. He fought in all the subsequent campaigns and at the final great battle of Waterloo. Again—he must have been getting a bit stiff by this time—he fought in the French cavalry at Sebastopol. I have not been able to trace him after 1902, when he still lived, having had the rare

PROLOGUE

distinction of living in three centuries. Of course such an instance as this must be unique, but it serves to make vivid the narrowness of the time span separating us from those stirring days of equally incredible splendor and ferocity.

My father, too, has told me of conversations he held while a young soldier stationed on St. Helena, with a fine old gentleman who had lived on the island all his life. He distinctly recalled that as a boy of twelve he had been taken, with his parents, to drive past the Longwood grounds, where they caught a glimpse of the Emperor Napoleon walking in the garden with another man. Once more, through such a linkage, time seems to telescope itself and one feels he has but to reach out and touch the actors—so close to us they have approached, and so impressive the illusion of actuality.

Napoleon had been but forty-six years old when his exile commenced. His vitality and physical vigor had been so impressive for the first three years that they excited comment from his many visitors and observers. Soon afterward, however, the realization of the hopelessness of his position, his ennui, and the cumulative ills of his sedentary existence bore him relentlessly down to his end. At age fifty-two he was dead, receiving temporary interment in a peaceful little valley he had discovered in his walks and had loved for its beauty and quiet. It was to be almost twenty years before France called him back to a more appropriate tomb in his onetime capital city.

Or so the histories attest, on the basis of what appear at first inspection to be sound evidential accounts.

It is the purpose of this book, however, to point out that these same documents are in actuality trying to tell us a quite different story—concerning the last years on St. Helena, at least. It will be suggested that if the accepted dogma be scrutinized with less

WHO LIES HERE?

myopic reverence and with a shrewder, more discriminating vision, a novel and startling concept at once leaps forth as not only a distinct possibility but as an exceedingly probable solution to a good many mysteries. For the attainment of this fresh and unbiased viewpoint no new revelations or disclosures of secret archives are required, but merely a reconsideration of the old and familiar records and of their origins, in a mood of intellectual courage. In addition a good deal of quite meaningless verbiage that has become integral to the story over the years—copied, one may suspect, by a succession of uncritical scribes, and by each a little enhanced—will be thrust aside and shown to be both false and misleading.

When this is done, carefully and conscientiously, I am confident that the reader will never again be as assured as in the past regarding the identity of the occupant of that massive sarcophagous beneath the dome of Les Invalides. I entertained my first doubts some twenty years ago, when strange and unaccountable incidents of the last three years of the St. Helena exile first drew themselves to my attention. Since then, by the accumulation of additional material, my early doubts have become more nearly a certainty: I am strongly disposed to believe that the tomb of Napoleon lies elsewhere in Europe, unknown to fame, and that the Invalides sepulchre is that of another—a most obscure but greatly loyal—soldier.

THOMAS G. WHEELER

Los Angeles, California

Part One
THE FURY FADES

> *Reasonable people do not realize to what exaltation the feeling of existence may attain: the heart dilates, the imagination takes an immense flight—one lives with FURY!*
> —BERLIOZ

> *There are few pains so grievous as to have seen, divined, or experienced how an exceptional man has missed his way, and collapsed.*
> —NIETZSCHE

W HEN IN the spring of 1814—his first abdication and the Treaty of Fontainebleau effected and become matters of history—Napoleon grimly started for the Mediterranean and his ridiculous little token kingdom of Elba, he had such small notion of continuing there for any length of time that he permitted a seemingly flippant remark to escape him: He would return with the violets, he had predicted; in plain language, by the spring of the next year. Eagerly that word was passed on from mouth to mouth among the faithful, and soon the catalogue of code words for the absent emperor was enriched by that of "Père Violette," which sent the cost of the bouquets spiraling in Paris. Disillusion with the restored Bourbons was mounting swiftly in the volatile capital, thence flooding out over the entire country to lift and revive the restless spirits of swarms of old soldiers and half-pay officers of the Empire.

No sooner arrived in his domain but the newly constituted monarch—apparently in the best of spirits and not in the least abashed by his recent misfortunes—hurled himself with all his old energy into the midst of a thousand projects and enterprises of vital concern to the economy and welfare of the sleepy island. He leaped from the encouragement of bee culture to the establishment of mulberry groves, from the design of an appropriate flag to the

WHO LIES HERE?

laying out of a system of new roads, from the importation of improved stock for cattle breeding to schemes of housing developments. Even a new opera house was ordained and the remodeling and fusing of some already existent buildings to constitute an imperial palace. Throughout all the great campaigns of the Empire, the place where Napoleon established his headquarters, where he slept—even for a night on the battlefield, though it might of necessity be but a wretched hut—was designated "the palace"; so it was to be on Elba, and still styled imperial, since he conceived that status to be irrevocably his by plebiscite of the French people. Apparently the European monarchs had come to the same conclusion about his right to the imperial title, for they had volunteered the clause in the treaty that guaranteed it to him even in exile.

Many of the improvements Napoleon brought about in the island's economy persist to this day—the roads, the industries, the foreign trade and commerce he shaped out for the long-term prosperity of the islanders, long cut off and in part isolated from the world of affairs and ideas and notions of progress. Indeed, they had been supplied, in return for their modest taxes grudgingly paid, with the services of a very high-priced man indeed: one whose industry had covered Europe with systems of canals, broad paved roads, modern harbors and every variety of great public works. This had been the other side of the medallion, one not as often regarded as the pictured reverse, painted in blood and the morbid coloring of decay and death. But the gentle Elbans were to know nothing of all that, for their minute foothold of land and rock afforded no scope for any part of such gigantic canvases as their new monarch was accustomed to employ in creating his appalling masterpieces.

Elba is only twenty miles by six; their king had found all Europe too small for him only a few months before.

THE FURY FADES

They went on, wonderingly, accepting the changes and developments and the promises of future prosperity—and objecting to the rising taxes, of course. They could not know that Napoleon was using his own funds to make these things possible—his private money and yet more he borrowed from the beautiful Pauline, the sister who loved him and was ever loyal. Both she and his mother—Madame Mère, the only other one of his family to stand by him in the disaster of his fortunes—came to live with him and to grace his modest court. The comings and goings of friends and relatives were, officially, unobserved and unnoted by the allied commissioners stationed on the island: As king, Napoleon's actions and the visitors he received were his own affair. In actuality, of course, his actions were subjected to the closest scrutiny and the gravest consideration of the European ministers who maintained their agents in Porto Ferraio, Elba's diminutive capital.

Napoleon had not been altogether forgotten.

However, to all appearances, he would seem to have forgotten Europe.

Month after month he continued to drive himself with his old relentless energy, building, organizing, reviewing his minuscule army. (For, in addition to the four hundred of his old soldiers he had been authorized to take with him, three hundred more had come of their own accord to be with their adored Emperor and to serve him in any humble capacity.) He built up a tiny navy from a few cargo vessels and fishing boats, finding among the islanders sufficiently skilled seamen to man them. As far as the world was able to determine, he was apparently content, amazingly cheerful, altogether resigned to his fate—so they proceeded gradually to forget about him, leaving him out of their calculations.

With him vanished, it was easy to begin to imagine the whole episode a sort of bad dream: the ceaseless battles and turbulence, the interminable casualty lists, the demonic will. It was gone like a

WHO LIES HERE?

vision of the night, and the titled refugees, the émigrés, the nobility of the older France who had fled to England to escape the menace of the revolution were streaming back with undiminished arrogance to reclaim their ancient charters.

Had these sanguine people had but a faint conception of what was hatching under that terrifying cocked hat they recalled so vividly—they conceived of him as a rural squire on nearby Elba immersed in petty pursuits—these and their kings and ministers gathered together in council at Vienna would have trembled in their polished jackboots and canceled their mounting dissensions and jealousies to form a common front. They were assembled in this Council of Vienna to recarve the map of Europe, to change Napoleon's boundaries, to regroup or to share the lesser states —and above all to demand of one another and of France in particular, as much money in reparations and penalties as the traffic might bear. Hence, most of the matter for dissension; already they were divided into parties, those having common interests or hatreds, and toward the end it seemed likely that actual warfare might break out at any moment. From their unedifying brawling it was apparent that Russia was to emerge as a new, dominating force; England, supreme on all the oceans and at the height of her economic power, continued to prevail over them, and her representative, the Duke of Wellington, was deferred to by all.

Napoleon, in actuality, had allowed himself a few weeks' vacation, that was all; those furious activities occupied his superficial faculties while his mind was at the kind of work most natural to it. Between himself and the spies of his enemies he had erected a screen that was both then and later on so perfectly efficient that it was never penetrated nor ever even suspected of having been created primarily for this essential purpose.

A precise technique of preparation for evasion suggests itself as one examines the historical account of the Emperor's Elban resi-

THE FURY FADES

dence; it becomes evident that almost from the beginning certain subtle, long-range plans were being initiated. The activities themselves were inconspicuous enough or sufficiently natural under the circumstances to arouse little or no suspicion in the breasts of local observers. And they could have been discontinued or reversed at any time, if changing attitudes had seemed to warrant it, without jeopardy to the plotter's condition or prospects. It is interesting and profitable to examine this technique and to observe its workings, for it is precisely the technique that Napoleon initiated at the very beginning of his later exile on St. Helena, in preparation for his second escape in 1818. He could well afford to employ it twice in succession because, as he understood quite well, his enemies had not in the least comprehended its beautiful simplicity and effectiveness—any more than in the glorious past they had been able to divine his battle strategies and the ineffable brilliance of campaign after campaign.

Naturally the removal of a closely guarded prisoner of war from the confines of such a diligently patroled fortress-island as St. Helena was to become would call for procedures radically different from those employed in the essentially straightforward departure, in his own ships, of the acknowledged "monarch" of Elba; nevertheless, it would have been utterly useless to have contemplated either venture without having first constructed the screening wall, an incredibly impervious device, that would enable the participants in both schemes to work without fear of interference or premature exposure.

On Elba there was but a minimum of discreet supervision to be neutralized—on St. Helena there would be an absolute maximum: physical space could hardly have been found for more. Yet from the governor and his hierarchy down through the entire garrison to the two English "gardeners" at the bottom, not one would ever be able to pierce that protective screen—the very same elaborately staged

WHO LIES HERE?

piece of flummery that was about to undo Sir Neil Campbell, the British Commissioner stationed on Elba. Napoleon required, in both instances, a relatively brief interval in which to appraise his new environment and circumstances: a strategic survey and consideration of the locale together with a specific appraisal of the minds and persons of his antagonists. Then, even if he had not by then determined what his ultimate plan was to be—Phase One of the operation was initiated, never to be relaxed. This was the erection of the protective screen, and it consisted of the creation, or rather of the continuation, of the imperial court.

One of the disarming beauties of this superbly effective device was its obvious folly—the pathetic megalomania of a humbled dictator and ruined warlord too engrossed in the memories of power and self-aggrandizement to be able to yield up its forms and trappings. All the world was amused when they read of this ridiculous business of Grand Marshals of the Imperial Palace, Grand Equerries, Imperial Chamberlains and the rest—and of the preposterous little fellow who threw away any correspondence not properly addressed to him as His Imperial Majesty. This Bonaparte was, it now became easy to perceive, little more than a clown after all, in spite of some military repute acquired in his very early days, and like all parvenus a presumptuous fellow to boot. Apparently he intended to insist on what he considered appropriate honors and observances from his guards and captors, the same deference from privileged guests as from the officers of his "household"—exactly those he had received at the palace of the Tuileries in the days of his usurpation. "Well, well—not too much there to concern us any longer!" was the European consensus when they read of these antics: "Fellow's still wrapped up in his dreams and posturings, his absurd protocol and rules of precedence: All this mad rigmarole of his petty and shabby imitation of a court!"

That was one aspect of the screen—it inspired the world to

THE FURY FADES

laughter and to the discounting of the principal actor as a pathetic buffoon or at the least a harmless posturer at the fringes of reality and no longer one to be taken into serious account by the marveling nations.

The serious truth of it was, however, that it was damnably effective, a perfect cover for any amount of secret activity within, more apt to the purpose than any other an exposed and helpless captive could possibly have devised for himself. Against it, both then and later, the fury of baffled jailers or of thwarted spies was to rage in vain—for who could dare to make so puerile a decree as to declare it a menace, or improper, or a treasonable defiance of the so-called Holy Alliance, the combined powers of Europe?

The entire household collaborated willingly with their master, spontaneously and happily entering into the roles accorded them in the arrangement; one and all they supported each other in their accustomed parts, combining to maintain the dignity and aloofness of their chieftain against any rude or indecorous activity from the Outside, from the Enemy. These last might find the situation irritating, at times something of a nuisance perhaps—those who without such restraints on their arrogance would have stormed without ceremony into the very bedroom of the fallen monarch had the way not been barred by energetically maintained customs, presences and pressures—up to and including the threat of firearms, had such measures ultimately been called for.

As a screen and a moat defensive then, it worked well. And like the legendary custom of later Englishmen, stationed in remote or barbarous lands, this "dressing for dinner" served also to maintain the exiles' morale in the face of alien suspicions or contemptuous regard.

Although it appeared that the intention of the allied powers had been to permit their distingushed prisoner unlimited freedom within the confines of the island, nevertheless, there was raised up against him almost from the beginning of his tenure a self-appointed jailer and indefatigable spy, against whom the new King was soon compelled to take defensive measures. This was Sir Neil Campbell, the British commissioner: a gallant soldier who bore the scars of several wounds received in the recent fighting. Both his nationality and military record at first recommended him in the Emperor's eyes, and it was not until several weeks had passed that he received evidence of Campbell's largely self-initiated career of spying.

It is a somewhat strange circumstance that on both Elba and St. Helena Napoleon was to encounter two such Englishmen as Sir Neil Campbell and Sir Hudson Lowe: the first merely the representative of the English crown, the second the official governor and jailer; each of them in his degree paranoiac, pathologically suspicious, brooding, preoccupied with the need for intensive spying and increasingly governed by the malignant demands of a peculiarly perverted obsessionary instinct. To Campbell's increasingly devious wrongheadedness his diary's pages bear sufficient witness, while all the world has long been made aware of Lowe's inherent afflictions. However, even if these men had been of normal disposition to start with—and there is plenty of evidence that Lowe at least was not—one might imagine that the proximity in which they were placed to the terrible object of their attentions would have been in itself sufficient to exacerbate any native instabilities, to bring out in each man evidences of his own paltriness or unworthy fears. To stand guard night and day over a military genius, whether voluntarily or assignedly, should be regarded as one of the most mentally hazardous of occupations!

Against these two men and their cohorts only one weapon was to be of any avail—defensively, at least: the "Brummagem Court," as it was contemptuously styled in Europe and in the British press. Ridiculous and vain, beyond doubt—but even in face of the

THE FURY FADES

ultimate malignity of St. Helena, as before in thwarting the clumsier efforts of the Elban spy ring, it stood to the very end unshakable and impenetrable.

First, there had been a period of disorganization and seeming aimlessness, as the French tentatively established homes for themselves and Napoleon himself cast about for suitable temporary quarters. During this period on Elba there was the minimum of difficulty or formality in obtaining access to the person of the Emperor, and the English commissioner was a frequent and welcome visitor at the royal residence. Napoleon had been impressed by what he had learned of the stability and inherent honesty of the better-class Englishman quite early in his career, and seems never to have entirely given up his conception in spite of repeated disillusionment. Later, on St. Helena, he was to be overcome with admiration for Sir Pulteny Malcolm, the British admiral in charge of the flotilla assigned to patrol the island. "There is the countenance of a typical Englishman," he told Count Bertrand, "as pleasant to regard as that of a pretty woman!" He was not wrong about Malcolm, as one may judge today from his portrait; but there were others. . . .

But as to Sir Neil Campbell, on Elba, in a comparatively brief space of time Napoleon had in hand indisputable evidence of the commissioner's tireless spying and of his regular reports to his government regarding any and all questionable activities of the French: ships of other nationalities that called at the little harbor, strangers who came and went, additions to the ranks of the little army coming from Italy as well as France, and the identities of sundry titled callers from foreign lands. It was obviously going to become necessary to restrict the opportunities of this English official to come at savory morsels of information—and in particular to gain ready access to the Emperor himself or to indulge

WHO LIES HERE?

himself, in the palace, with his habit of shrewd questioning and close observation. The thing was simply effected: With the occupance of the newly completed Mulini Palace, ample and appropriately compartmented, there came the organization of the Imperial Court and the installation of all the old procedures and formalities. The officials were always splendidly uniformed, the chamberlains and their pages properly garbed in the imperial colors of green and gold, while impressive figures of Grenadiers of the Old Guard stood on sentry duty within and without, bayonets fixed.

Soon thereafter Colonel Campbell began to find himself increasingly *persona non grata* at the palace, but this situation was gradually effected in a manner that could cause him little offense, since the rules were maintained for all would-be interviewers alike—and beyond that because his government had not officially sanctioned his probing and prying, although they appeared happy enough to take advantage of it. His quite honest musings over his new disadvantages are somewhat ingenuously set forth in his diary of late 1814:

> My access to Napoleon has for some time past been so much less than at first as to afford me very little opportunity for personal observation: and besides, the etiquette of a sovereign and court were studiously adhered to. So that during the last few months our intercourse has been continued under different feelings on both sides, although no expression to that effect was ever pronounced by either of us; and when he did grant me an interview he always received me with the same apparent courtesy as formerly.

That mildly puzzled passage would seem to have set forth the

THE FURY FADES

situation rather adequately. But the assiduous colonel had yet a trick or two up his own sleeve, it appeared. By taking a periodic vacation on the Italian mainland he was enabled to enjoy the mineral baths at Lucca (where the waters helped assuage the increasing stiffening of his wounds), and to visit Leghorn and Florence also—there renewing certain amorous as well as military contacts. On his return to the island, court etiquette demanded that he promptly seek an interview with the Emperor, to pay his respects, as it were, and to give an account of himself. Such permission could not be refused him, of course, and thus the ingenious officer got his relaxation at Florence *and* the prized interview at the palace—not at all a bad arrangement for him. "Of late," his journal continues, "he has evidently wished to surround himself with great forms of court, as well to preserve his own consequence in the eyes of the Italians as to keep me at a distance—for I could not transgress on these without the probability of an insult, or on my part the proffer of servile adulation inconsistent with my sentiments."

There is a good deal more to the same effect, while the mounting frustration and anger of the thwarted spy become more evident with each entry. For lack of being able any longer to go directly to the heart of local affairs, the colonel's attentions were necessarily forced outward to such peripheral sources as the docks, the idlers, soldiery and fishermen. He did not neglect his consulates and other countries' representatives on the mainland, where he maintained a chain of casual informers, and these—and Napoleon's larger and more efficient chain—threw dust in each other's eyes while they went on with their endless plotting. Nevertheless, under the cover of this shield the commissioner so deplored, not only was the actual removal of the French from Elba actually carried out, faultlessly and without any interference whatever —neither had it been anticipated by any of the European governments or their agents, despite the continual coming and going of their observers and all the gentry of dubious enterprise who frequented the island.

At all events, that is how it was worked, and we have the testimony of a good run-of-the-mill would-be spy and ambitious jailer as to its efficiency. It is well to note that Napoleon's escape was carried out in the face of many difficulties not at once apparent. For ten months his daily words and actions, even the most innocuous, were noted down, analyzed and reported in detail to the assembled heads of state at the Congress of Vienna. It would be by no means a simple task to blind temporarily or render immobile this mass of anonymous observers, spies, saboteurs and plain assassins, then embark several hundred men with all their arms, stores and supplies, not to speak of the cavalry horses and their fodder, for a destination that had to be kept secret from everyone until the very last moment. It is obvious that without that impregnable system of court protocol and regulation it would have been all but impossible to bring off—particularly in light of the persistent curiosity of the ubiquitous Sir Neil, his Brittanic Majesty's Elban representative.

This last, the most pressing of his problems, was handled for him very nicely by his beautiful sister Pauline, who seduced the amorous colonel into an implied rendezvous in Florence. Whether it was ever kept is not recorded—but at least Campbell was gone when the Emperor sailed, passing safely through the patrol of British frigates supposed to be circling the island and the waters northward that divided the island from the French coast.

So Napoleon set forth unopposed into the declining sun of the Hundred Days, and the somber shadows of Waterloo: so many events and transitions, so many calamities and deaths, all crowded together into that brief, foredoomed postscript to Empire! On March 20, 1815, the Emperor had returned to France—with the

THE FURY FADES

violets, as he had promised; by June 18 he had fought his final great battle—and lost; on October 17 he and his forlorn suite disembarked, the military prisoners of England, onto the stone quay of Jamestown, St. Helena—the strongest, remotest, least assailable and the loneliest of all the world's prisons.

The technicalities involved in sentencing France's ex-Emperor to lifetime imprisonment and exile were of a considerable magnitude, involving nice interpretations of English law as well as repudiation of determined efforts by Liberals to effect, by appeal to parliamentary procedure, Napoleon's release—or at least his confinement in England as a sort of privileged country squire, as he had requested when he surrendered. There was a strong body of legal opinion that declared it was distinctly illegal to imprison Napoleon now that the war was over and he had voluntarily surrendered himself. The whole matter might have come to trial had a certain prominent attorney been able to serve a subpoena on Lord Keith, the British admiral responsible for Napoleon's custody; with considerable agility that distinguished seaman evaded the lawyer, dodging from ship to ship in Plymouth harbor. Had the subpoena been served, Napoleon would have been obliged to appear in court in his own defense—and the outcome of such a process can only be speculated on, for the sporting element in the English character was swinging public opinion strongly to the side of the fallen Emperor, as many articles and letters in the public press indicated.

The British cabinet were in almost constant session, clearing away legal obstacles and receiving regular communications from the European ministers now gathered in Paris. These latter, undeterred by any legal scruples, produced between them the Convention of Paris, signed on August 2, 1815, and a copy was at once sent to London. One of its clauses ran:

WHO LIES HERE?

> Bonaparte's custody is especially entrusted to the British government. The choice of the place and of the measures which can best secure the object of the present stipulation is reserved to His Britannic Majesty. The imperial courts of Austria and of Russia and the royal court of Prussia are to appoint commissioners to proceed and to abide at the place which His Britannic Majesty shall have assigned for the residence of Napoleon Bonaparte, and who, without being responsible for his custody, will assure themselves of his presence. His Most Christian Majesty (Louis XVIII) is to be invited, in the name of the above-mentioned courts, to send in like manner a French Commissioner to the place of detention of Napoleon Bonaparte.

This was the authority of Europe, had Britain felt herself in need of it, for the imprisonment of the Emperor. Doubtless the English ministers noted the total lack of any reference to the sharing of costs: from the first it was tacitly assumed that they would be met, as most of the costs of the wars had been met, by the British only. The act of exile began:

> Whereas His Royal Highness the Prince Regent acting in the name and on behalf of His Majesty has been pleased to command that General N. Buonaparte and the French persons attending him should be detained on the island of St. Helena . . . this is to warn all inhabitants and other persons on this island from aiding and abetting hereafter in any way whatsoever the escape of the said General and that of any of the French persons with him, and to interdict most pointedly the holding

THE FURY FADES

of any communication or correspondence with them . . . any person presuming to act in violation of this ordinance will be immediately sent off the island to be further punished as the circumstances appear to deserve.

The island of St. Helena was a possession of the East India Company, one of a long chain of islands and ports established by them for coaling, watering and victualing stations for their ships and the convenience of their passengers on the long voyages between Empire ports. The precise relationship of this mighty company to the Empire sponsoring it is much too complicated to consider here; they had an astounding degree of autonomy and self-determination, owned their own fleet of armed merchant and passenger vessels, policed India with their own army, and operated very much as an independent nation might do, consistent with perfect loyalty to the British throne. It had been necessary, therefore, for the latter to obtain permission from the East India Company for the use of their island as a place of detention for Napoleon. Their agreement began in these terms:

Whereas Napoleon Buonaparte having surrendered himself to the Government of this country, His Majesty's ministers, deeply sensible of the high importance of effectually securing the person of a man whose conduct has proved so fatal to the happiness of the world, and judging that the island of St. Helena is eminently fitted to answer that purpose, have proposed to us that he shall be placed there under a system of government adapted to serve the end in view. . . . As the East India Company hold the principle of rendering their means and faculties, on all practical occasions,

WHO LIES HERE?

conducive to the national interests and objects, we have not thought ourselves at liberty to decline a compliance in so remarkable a case.

Then followed the harassing restrictions devised by the local officials of the company, for it would be they who, until the appointment of a permanent governor and his arrival in St. Helena, would actually be responsible for Napoleon's safe custody. These and—by a thoughtful provision of the British government—Sir George Cockburn, admiral of the St. Helena squadron destined to patrol the island. Admiral Cockburn was a man well known to Americans, yet despite the evil fame he had acquired by the burning of Washington two years previously, he was in actuality a first-class naval officer and carried out a difficult task with fairness and firmness.

In spite of these documents and the instructions of the European ministers, Britain continued to play it safe as to the legality of her actions in exiling Napoleon. First Commons enacted a law specifically authorizing the nation to carry out and maintain the imprisonment as contemplated—and yet another (on the advice of an apprehensive legal counsel) granting the government immunity from any charge of illegality that might be brought against it in the future! After that, without doubt, the ministers must have experienced considerable relief, although articles denouncing their behavior continued to appear in the press, their theme being that the incarceration for life of the deposed Emperor was in the highest degree improper and unprecedented. They agreed with him in principle, that he had voluntarily come aboard the British warship *Bellerophon* to request England's hospitality, had sent a letter to the Prince Regent so stating, and had been forcibly seized in a gross breach of faith. Without doubt there was some right on both sides—but the stronger prevailed.

THE FURY FADES

Napoleon's exile, then, was devised by the allied nations of Europe assembled in Paris personified in their ministers and rulers. Their authority derived from the fact that when he had "illegally" returned from Elba to France, they had jointly declared him an outlaw—that is, one beyond the law's succor and subject to their ukase without possibility of appeal. To England, acknowledged mistress of the world's seas, they entrusted the matter of his security and restraint, and all of them had such a remote place as St. Helena in mind for this purpose: There were those among them who would have suggested the Emperor's execution, but a healthy consideration for public opinion—which they well realized was becoming sullen and resentful as the lower orders began to realize that the reforms of the great revolution were steadily being nullified—kept them from openly considering this drastic solution.

In turn England obtained the right to use her East India Company's distant base, the company's officials staying on to devise and ordain the rules of Napoleon's restraint (as guided directly from the ministry of Lord Bathurst, Colonial Foreign Office, London). Within a few months a British governor would be appointed, and thereafter he would be responsible for the creation of any further regulations that might be required to control the activity of the Emperor and his French "family"—his companions and staff who had elected to accompany him into his exile.

From the battleship *Bellerophon*, where he had lived since his surrender in Rochefort, Napoleon, in company with the French who had crossed the Channel at the same time, was transferred to the *Northumberland*—a similarly aging warship but one considered capable of the long and arduous voyage they were now embarking on. In company with them were four armed brigs and three transports bearing troops for the reinforcement of the island's

WHO LIES HERE?

garrison. They were to arrive at their destination, after an extremely trying journey, on October 17, 1815—only four months after the forever-intriguing battle of Waterloo had written an abrupt *finis* to the imperial story.

Throughout the voyage the French had been deluding themselves as to the nature of their future home, their status and the conditions of their new existence—imagining for themselves, in more optimistic moments, something comparable to the pleasant environment and the comforts of Elba; they were to be immediately and most rudely undeceived, and the first sight of St. Helena provided a brutally abrupt awakening. (One of the ladies, perhaps Madame Montholon, is reported to have observed, "The island looks as though the devil had shit it in flying from one world to another!")

But even before they had left Plymouth harbor the new, sterner attitude of the British was being made evident in many minor ways and in other ways that carried ugly implications of things yet to be brought about—Napoleon, for example, was reduced officially to the rank of general in the usage prescribed for his captors. (When he first received a written communication thus addressed, he exploded: "General Bonaparte?" he cried incredulously. "The last I heard of him was at the Pyramids!") He never yielded to this attempt to humble him, and up to the last rejected all such messages—sending them spinning from the open window to be recovered, unread, by gardener or British orderly officer. Communication between the governor and himself could be effected, therefore, only through the intermediary of the Grand Marshal. And because invitations to official balls, military revues or the annual races were by courtesy addressed to him directly, and therefore inscribed with the inadmissible and galling "General Bonaparte," Napoleon was unable to accept any such invitations himself even though he encouraged his staff to do so.

THE FURY FADES

In England all their money (except some concealed by the valets in money belts) and certain of their weapons were taken from them; the money, they were informed, would be used to help defray their living costs—one of the few cases on record where prisoners were asked to pay for their own support! Other indications were not lacking either—the uncompromising manner, the firm and resolute attitude of officialdom, the minimal deference—that the French were to find their captivity more rigorous than they had anticipated. Among Napoleon's first acts, after his future domicile had been decided on and set into some approach to order and convenience, was the reestablishment of the Imperial Court structure, the great value of which he had demonstrated to himself during his first imprisonment on Elba—Elba, where he had been a King still, still entitled to the style of "His Imperial Majesty," in the spring of that very same year! Galling, indeed; yet he had once observed in his cynical fashion, "Better a live drummer than a dead general!" Napoleon was very much alive and, as always, pleased with life and its endless possibilities.

There were, however, many disheartening aspects of this new existence. The only house that could be modified sufficiently to accommodate them all, aside from Plantation House itself, the governor's luxurious mansion, was a deplorably rundown and rambling affair called Longwood. This structure, a part of which had recently been in use as a cattle barn, was located high on a windswept plateau continually exposed to the moisture-laden southeast trades, quite bare of trees or other growth. It was reputed to be the dampest and least desirable place on the island, its owner living there only during the summer months. It was brought into somewhat better condition, consolidated and extended a little, by sailors from the *Northumberland*'s crew who also finished it off with plenty of paint—in the traditional manner of seamen. It is of interest to note that Plantation House—two-storied, spacious,

WHO LIES HERE?

with acres of fine lawn and gardens—had been at first designated as the future home of the French; that, however, would have meant that the governor and his staff would have had to discover other quarters far less gratifying. The matter was conveniently lost sight of.

From the beginning the Emperor's new residence was abominably crowded and wretchedly inconvenient, even though General Bertrand with his wife and child refused to move in, and found a small house for themselves about a mile and a quarter distant. Today it is the property of the French government, who have restored it to its original condition and had its original furniture duplicated or, in some instances, recovered from homes or local secondhand stores. The description of the primitive cooking arrangements is next to incredible, when the elaborate nature of the meals served, the frequent pastries and confections, is recollected. It was, moreover, a very large household—during the first three years, at least—and numbered at the beginning about fifty-four men, women and children, the majority of these classified as "the service," including valets, doormen, grooms, ushers, cooks and servants of all descriptions. The number varied continually, owing to local additions and defections. There was included also at a later period the British orderly officer and his aides; he lived in his own quarters on the property, and his duty was to report instantly (by means of an old semaphore signaling device) any news whatever of his ward's significant activity or even indisposition, as well as to determine daily the actual presence, as demonstrated to his sight, of the Emperor in person.

There were also fifteen British soldiers, lent as servants and gardeners, but the most significant of the "outsiders" in residence at Longwood was the Irish surgeon, Dr. O'Meara. When Napoleon had crossed to England in the *Bellerophon,* he had been accompanied by his own physician, a Dr. Maingault, who had

THE FURY FADES

expressed the wish to continue as his doctor no matter what the Fates should decree; however, at the mention of St. Helena for his future abode he lost his enthusiasm and withdrew. In his place Napoleon was served by the ship's physician, a young man of thirty-three named Barry O'Meara, who impressed him favorably with his high spirits and proficiency, as well as by his ability to speak Italian. The English were amenable to the idea of having him transferred to St. Helena as Napoleon's doctor, at the same time retaining him on the Navy rolls in order to preserve his pay and seniority as an officer. His relations with the Emperor were most cordial, the Emperor finding himself at ease with the facile Irishman and amused by his stories; he came at last to repose considerable trust in the doctor's integrity. Professionally O'Meara was sound enough, as doctors were estimated in those days, but he was possibly too jovial, somewhat indiscreet in his communications regarding matters observed or discussed at Longwood.

His was a privileged position, critical indeed, and it is generally agreed that he may have carried to Plantation House a good deal of information of the sort the governor was only too anxious to obtain. His revelations, however, were insufficient for the sharpened appetite of the governor, who certainly made improper proposals to O'Meara regarding further betrayals of the Emperor's trust, and the entire matter became a *cause célèbre* when, in due course, it was brought to light.

At any rate, these Longwood people were to be the only tools immediate to Napoleon's hand; if with these he could not effect the first essential crack in the iron ring drawn around him, then indeed he might well resign himself to the death of boredom and desuetude his captors had designed. But over and beyond the aid of these willing servants he had at his command the great mind that all the world had learned was strung to its keenest and most terrifying pitch of intensity when all seemed lost, and lesser men

WHO LIES HERE?

fled the field. The greatest mystery of the St. Helena story is in fact this: How is it possible to believe that the most brilliant and successful soldier of all time—the statesman who at his prime had shown more capacity, shrewdness, and understanding than Metternich, Talleyrand and Castlereagh all rolled into one—should henceforward sit quiescent in his grim Atlantic solitude, bandying shrewish words with the pathological governor until at last he succumbed to the self-generated toxins of idleness and despair?

If Napoleon were truly the giant history proclaims him and his deeds confirm, it would have been an obvious impossibility for him to have existed and died inert in that drab and hopeless environment, the object of the world's leering curiosity or contemptuous indifference. The totality of such a picture is inconsistent with its parts, like a fake circus mermaid contrived by sewing a fish's tail to the body of a monkey. The line of junction, though cunningly scaled and concealed, can yet be discerned by the curious.

Instead of giving way to despair he proceeded almost at once to establish again the elements of an Imperial Court—first things came first.

The Grand Marshal of the palace was to be, as on Elba, General Count Bertrand—a tall, grave and serious man who had been trained as an army engineer, but who had risen to the command of an army corps before becoming Grand Marshal at the Tuileries. His loyalty was unquestioned, his patience almost unlimited, and he was without doubt ideally suited for his function—which was to serve as something like a majordomo combined with a secretary. He was married to a lady usually conceded to have been the most attractive on the island, despite an oversized nose. She had been born Fanny Dillon, of a well-known Anglo-Irish family, and spoke perfect English. This accomplishment was of considerable use in

THE FURY FADES

negotiating certain contacts of great value to the exiles, and in aiding in the popularization of the French among the more reticent of the islanders. The Bertrands and their son Arthur lived remote from the other French in their house at Hutt's Gate.

Grand Chamberlain of the palace was General Count Montholon whose full title under the old French regime had been Marquis de Montholon-Sémonville. His past career, like that of Albine, Madame Montholon, had been characterized by a good deal of so-called irregularity: frantic opportunism, shady financial areas, swift changing of sides as the Empire's fortunes fluctuated. Perhaps it is because of these traits, rendering them so very human in our regard, that the Montholons are found to be quite the most interesting people at Longwood—after the Emperor, of course. Like most such people they were good company, obliging, accommodating, kindly, and Napoleon enjoyed them both. Because General Bertrand was older and more reserved, it was noticed that he was gradually being replaced in the Emperor's affections and confidences by the more affable and likable Montholon: this was to produce tensions and violent resentments later, in particular between the two ladies. These two men—Bertrand and Montholon—were the only members of the staff to stay until the end, and therefore their memoirs—with those of the valet, Marchand—are the only complete ones of the exile; it is from them that we derive the entire body of knowledge we possess regarding life within Longwood's walls.

The Grand Equerry or Master of the Stables was General Count Gourgaud, a very young, impetuous and emotional artillery officer who had been aide-de-camp to the Emperor and a distinguished soldier. Wifeless, he was to find life on the island unusually trying, for his was an ardent temperament; his sometimes painfully frank diary describes his amatory excursions in Jamestown in

WHO LIES HERE?

explicit detail. Although Jamestown was designated the capital of St. Helena it was actually the only town there was, and it boasted but the one central street that ended at the harbor.

The fourth and last member of the staff, as one may designate Napoleon's titled companions, was Marie-Joseph-Emmanuel Augustin Dieudonné de Las Cases, Marquis de Las Cases, lord of la Caussade, Puylaurens, Lamothe and Dourne. He was a modest and retiring little man who made a poor showing in the midst of these military figures and their showy uniforms. He had been one of those aristocratic *émigrés* who had early accepted Napoleon's invitation to return to France and assist the Empire with their talents. To accompany the exiles he threw up career and fortune, leaving his wife behind—but thoughtfully bringing his young son Emmanuel for his secretary; this poor boy was almost ruined in health by the drudgery of hours of transcriptions of his father's scribbled notes, taken down at white heat from the Emperor's dictation. There is little doubt that Las Cases came to St. Helena with that one thought paramount—to obtain the material for a book whose great appeal to the public would bring him handsome rewards; despite that, his loyalty and enthusiasm for Napoleon were without doubt genuinely felt emotions, and his hero worship sincere.

These then were the companions whom fate and chance had provided for the fallen Emperor—and for each other, as well. In the close quarters to which they of necessity habituated themselves frictions would inevitably arise—resentments, jealousies, exacerbated feelings, intensified by the realization of their isolation from the active world, the absence of hope in their prospects for the years to come. It seems that the Montholons alone were able to keep all this to themselves and to devote themselves to what was really their primary function—that of being amiable companions to Napoleon, supporting him in his disaster and helping to make tolerable the years that stretched monotonously before him. For

THE FURY FADES

this realistic viewpoint and its always-kindly demonstration they were to be more richly rewarded than any others of the staff—even as they, beyond a shadow of doubt, had planned. The laborer is worthy of his hire, and Napoleon had always been willing to pay well for what he required most.

The "service" need only be mentioned as they come, a few only, to play their roles in the island story and to carry out the parts assigned them in working out the grand plot already beginning to preoccupy their master—for there is reason to believe that from the first his restless mind was grappling with the problem of escape, and that the broad outlines at least were taking tentative form there. That the task he had set himself would be no easy nut to crack Napoleon was of course fully aware—it would be a vastly more complicated performance than Elba, and one requiring, of necessity, a much longer period of time to arrange. It must have afforded that master strategist a good deal of pleasure, in after years, to contemplate its perfections, the smooth progression of each essential step. And the end product: a clean escape that no one—least of all his immediate captors—suspected! The prisoner seemingly still present and his body, ultimately, safely interred, with every mouth permanently sealed for the best of reasons! And beyond all, the great Napoleonic legend—rounded off and completed in the finest poetic tradition—launched by his lieutenants to be eternally propagated and enhanced by the worshippers of glory!

There were to be no loose ends, of course, to attract premature attention—neither then nor in the centuries to come, for that matter; all was to be left proper and seemly and the whole presented for the endorsement of history and the consecration of glory. Having in mind the grossly hampered life-style of his Longwood existence, this clandestine performance is without doubt Napoleon's *chef d'oeuvre*. It was not, of course, absolutely

WHO LIES HERE?

perfect, since nothing humanly contrived can be—there were to be enough "loose ends," after all, so that a thing so artistically devised might not remain forever unacknowledged and unenjoyed.

Although the French had found the conditions of their exile unpleasant from the beginning, it was not until the arrival of the newly appointed governor in April of 1816 that their trials really commenced, and the severity of the British government's intentions were made clear. It almost seemed that even before Sir Hudson Lowe had landed he had formed a personal antipathy for his prospective prisoner amounting almost to hatred. This, however, was virtual normalcy in Sir Hudson, it was soon to appear, regarding his relations with most of those people who were not his superiors in rank or status—and there were to be few indeed of these on St. Helena. In order to make sure of this, his government had conferred on him the "local" rank of lieutenant general—and its appropriate pay as well, together with as much again in living allowances. When he returned to England in 1821, he ventured to apply for confirmation of this rank, no doubt believing his endurance contest with the Emperor had well merited it; the Prince Regent, however, gave him a cold handshake and turned abruptly away with a promise of the first *colonelcy* that became vacant! It would appear the Emperor had been there before him, the unremitting efforts of the helpless-seeming prisoner already beginning to take their toll, influencing lives and destinies, as they may still be said to do to this day.

Lowe was undistinguished in appearance, his countenance strongly marked by mean and vindictive emotions: "A hangman's face!" as Napoleon described it succinctly. His military career had been as undistinguished as his person, evidenced in the fact that at the age of forty-two he had attained only the rank of colonel in an age when great opportunities for promotion (and these wholly due

THE FURY FADES

to the activities of the man he had come to guard!) had been plentiful indeed. For this post he had been almost "kicked upstairs," it would appear, since the Duke of Wellington had had him removed from his staff just prior to Waterloo. It is generally agreed that during his tenure of the governorship he rapidly succumbed to a magnificent anxiety neurosis, coupled with plentiful manifestations of paranoia—all of this brought about, beyond doubt, by the ingenious machinations of his supposedly resourceless prisoner.

Napoleon had privately looked forward to his first meeting with Lowe; a great deal was to depend on his impressions of the governor, on his intuitive appraisal of the man and his character. Hitherto he had had to contend only with the coldly neutral attitude of Admiral Cockburn, supreme commander of the local forces, in the interim. No doubt the Emperor sensed already that he was destined for an uncompromising regime of discipline and harassment, in an environment where his famous personal charm could have little effect in ameliorating the attitude of his custodians. That, should it turn out to be the case, could best be rebutted by the stiffly maintained defense of his Imperial Court—a firm wall, on which he congratulated himself, against prospective outrages or uncouth intrusions on his privacy. Or, as circumstances might dictate, it could be relaxed at will in favor of selected persons—even discarded altogether if it should turn out to be unnecessary for the confrontation with a possibly easygoing and affable governor.

It was operating with full force however, on the morning of April 16, 1816, when Sir Hudson for the first time—and most rashly—presented himself at Longwood. He had merely galloped up, without obtaining from the Grand Marshal the customary permission to call. A prisoner to send an invitation to his jailer? Preposterous! Up he rode, with his mounted suite, in the midst of

WHO LIES HERE?

a heavy downpour and at the unreasonable hour of nine in the morning, demanding to see "General Bonaparte," forsooth.

Naturally Napoleon gave orders not to admit him—and thus the endless feud was initiated. Lowe was instructed by the Grand Marshal to call at four o'clock of the following day. He apologized [!], and when he kept his appointment was duly received with proper formality: all four of the French officers in full dress, staff in livery of green and gold, candlelight gleaming on the abundance of fine silver. To quote Forsyth, Lowe's biographer and chief apologist, "From the first moment of seeing Lowe, Napoleon conceived a dislike for him, and this soon ripened into aversion." It was felt mutually, beyond doubt. In 1821, standing at the death-bed of his erstwhile prisoner, Lowe dared to "forgive" him, describing him as "his and England's greatest enemy," after having vented his spleen on the helpless object of his envious resentment for more than five dreary years.

Very shortly, however, matters were brought to a head; on August 18 of Lowe's first year he and the Emperor engaged in a final violent quarrel at Longwood, in the presence of Admiral Malcolm, who had succeeded Cockburn in the command of the local fleet. Lowe was never again to see his charge in life, never to be permitted to enter his home until he lay dead, in formal state, within.

It is difficult to believe that Napoleon did not deliberately create this prompt breach with the governor. The violent denunciation of some other, done, apparently, in the heat of a towering passion and with indescribable menace, was one of the Emperor's stock productions—he had, just before the rupture of the Peace of Amiens, so behaved to the British Ambassador at the Tuileries palace before the entire court. All report him as virtually insane with rage as he strode from the room—but just outside he was

THE FURY FADES

laughing heartily as he recounted the Englishman's discomfiture: merely a matter of policy, one of his techniques. It is likely that having by that time met Lowe a number of times, he had been able to make an accurate appraisal of his character and to learn all that he required to know regarding the future policy of Plantation House with respect to Longwood. In the past he had secretly estimated and correctly calculated the natures of much more complex and important men—either rejecting them at once or disarming them swiftly by an exercise of that personal fascination he understood so well how to employ. With such an insecure, weak, and readily flattered personality as Hudson Lowe presented, it would have been for the Emperor simplicity itself to have effectively fascinated and dominated that haunted man, thereby rendering existence on the harsh island much more tolerable for himself and his companions in exile. Obviously that was not what the Emperor wished to achieve.

Part of his purpose, as can now be perceived, was the furtherance of that legend which should adhere to his name forever—a legend in which his already famous career should form the body eternal, but to which his sacrificial extinction, there in the waste of waters amidst his inveterate enemies, should provide the sacred halo, the nimbus of unearthly flame. Prometheus crucified on his lonely rock—that great one who had brought down the fire of fame and glory to his ungrateful people! The mighty heart broken by the incessant jabs and pinpricks of his captors, by the indifference of his unworthy subjects—". . . the French people I have loved so well." This was a good part of his purpose; the rest of it was, and remained, to go away from there: inconspicuously and forever. To free himself permanently from the rule or domination of any other man, or nation. To shake off such names as "prisoner," or "General Bonaparte." "I only know how to command," he had stated once,

WHO LIES HERE?

and his career attested to the truth of that statement; he simply did not possess the faculty of subservience, of being a prisoner, of being a prisoner of such a man as Hudson Lowe.

The second step then, after the establishment of the Imperial Court, was to break immediately and irrevocably with the governor—to insult and demean that individual so thoroughly before his aides that his reappearance at Longwood would be unthinkable. After that the underlings could be held at bay without difficulty by the regular workings of protocol. Thus, it eventuated: Another essential phase of the plan had been conceived and carried out successfully. With the unacceptable governor eliminated from his calculations —regarding intrusions and invasions, at least, and personal interferences with members of the service and annoying liberties infringing on the precious privacy he required—all that had to be guarded against were the spies. Having a few of these of his own at large, and these no amateurs in the profession, he was well aware of the identities of most of the governor's agents, and of how to protect his own household against them.

Up to this significant period the French had been domiciled on St. Helena for almost eleven months—all of them charged with a lively resistance and characterized by a leitmotif of complaint and dissatisfaction. Beneath this frequently stormy surface, however, there flowed a steady and purposeful current of obscure activity —directed, in the first place, toward the creation of a nearly worldwide system of communications. The bickering and battling between Longwood and the governor's staff served well to distract the attention of the latter from what was going on under the very noses of the watchers retained by Lowe and the military and naval outposts he daily supervised. The never-ceasing shower of complaints from the French concerned themselves with the inadequate

THE FURY FADES

and primitive nature of the lodgings provided them, with the meagerness and inferior quality of the supplies, with the increasingly circumscribed areas of the island beyond which the Emperor might not venture unless accompanied by a British officer—and finally, with Lowe's inability to meet the cost (or so he stated) of Longwood's catering on the amount of money authorized by Lord Bathurst.

Had each of these points been satisfactorily settled, there is no doubt that yet others would have been created at once to replace them; a constant dissension was precisely what the French required for their purposes—a practice today referred to as "keeping the opponent off balance." One can almost feel pity for the perpetually frustrated Sir Hudson as it is seen how he was subtly managed and manipulated: first driven into frenzied rages and yelling of mighty threats, then reduced to wonderment and the verge of tears; again roused to vindictive action, lashing out at aides and scribes—even at Lady Lowe herself. It is not without reason that he has been spoken of as "the real martyr of St. Helena."

Could it possibly have been otherwise? On one hand the uninspired and plodding soldier—painstaking, pettifogging, unimaginative and unsure of the exact propriety of any one of his actions or decrees; forever rewriting and revising his orders and then destroying them; beginning all over again—then starting up in the middle of the night, maddened with anxiety, to gallop up to Longwood and a try for some shred of evidence—no matter what—that would indicate that Napoleon was still there and his own job yet secure; returning to issue and later to countermand all sorts of new orders having to do with ridiculous and petty matters as well as a few more serious ones, in order to try to regulate and curb that covertly rebellious activity he seems to have sensed, in a limited way, from the beginning.

And on the other side? The actual, physical presence of the

WHO LIES HERE?

greatest soldier-administrator the world has known; a mind among the most superior, a true genius; a master statesman, fertile in strategies, swift to pounce on his enemy's weakness and to seize the initiative. Literally a paralyzing presence, as so many kings and field marshals had learned for themselves during the previous twenty years!

Under such circumstances, if the Emperor required until the latter half of 1818 to effect his departure from the rock prison, it was conceivably because political considerations in the world at large, and in Europe particularly, were unfavorable. He bided his time—the proper time, as in the opening of a battle. Another reason the arrangements for escape could not be completed more rapidly was the obvious one of distance, of the island's remoteness: The ocean voyage between St. Helena and a Continental port required on an average six or seven weeks—the passage of the *Northumberland,* bringing the French to the island, had involved nearly nine, for the cumbersome square-rigged ships of the time were ever at the whim of adverse winds or turbulent seas. Accordingly the carrying out of complex instructions, step by step, the messages sent and received at such infrequent intervals—and sometimes necessarily miscarrying, or being found by the recipients to be impracticable or out of tune with local reality—was enormously time-consuming and frustrating. At last it must have been obvious to the Longwood circle that this unsure, protracted method of communication by letters would never answer their purpose—a better way had to be found.

Then, too, the opportunities for getting their mail off the island and of receiving the replies directed to them were not as frequent—and the technique not so simple—as could be wished. In theory, of course, such things were impossible: All letters from the prisoners (so ran Lord Bathurst's dictate) were to be handed unsealed to the governor for his perusal and final decision. Their

THE FURY FADES

incoming mail was similarly opened and studied, and such items often supplied Lowe with delightful opportunities to delay their delivery, to "lose" them, or to confiscate any item that might appeal to him. In addition to all this, intimate letters to Napoleon from his mother, or important ones from other relatives, first passed through the British minister's hands in London before being sent on, if he approved them, for Lowe's consideration at the local level. Sometimes the contents of such letters became broadcast about the island, as Napoleon had directly charged to Lowe's face in the presence of Admiral Malcolm, during that furious and final interview.

Such was the practice ordained by officialdom for the supervision of communications between the exiles and the world beyond. The practice that soon prevailed, however, even in the face of the governor's spy network, which covered the entire island, including every petty shop or bordello in Jamestown, was another thing altogether. As General Gourgaud was later to comment to British ministers, there are few doors that enough money cannot unlock—and of this commodity Napoleon commanded enough for all such needs, at the least. Enough he had, as is now known, despite his specious protests of poverty and the well-publicized selling of a large part of his sumptuous silver service in Jamestown—"for lack of the food to put on it!" as the devious Cipriani, the Emperor's footman, chief spy and secret counselor, so plaintively asserted to the interested natives. The effect of that story, when it got about in Europe, was at once to raise up a new wave of sympathy for the abased and abused prisoner, and another of denunciation of the parsimonious British government. This represented a masterstroke in the unremitting warfare the Emperor was waging with his conquerors, employing only such poor weapons as he had available. And it was typical of the great pains devoted to the consideration of every petty detail. In sum they

WHO LIES HERE?

were to contribute richly to the substance of the Great Legend, and the sound judgment of the master plotter is hardly to be questioned in view of the results he obtained. Incidentally, it is worth recording in this connection that Gourgaud later on revealed that just prior to the sacrifice of this splendid silver service Napoleon had been in receipt of "a large sum in gold"!

But—to paraphrase that general once again, it was not even necessary that Naopleon should have any considerable sum in his actual possession—obviously a simple chit signed by him would be honored almost anywhere in the world, and for any amount up to and including millions of francs: by Prince Eugène, his son-in-law in Italy, for example, or in London by the banking firm of Andrews, Street and Parker. In Paris the banker Lafitte held more than three million francs in trust for the Emperor—and there was yet Joseph, his brother, onetime king of Spain and the wealthiest of all the clan, a staunch ally in America. So there was money available in abundance both at home and abroad for rewarding any of the underpaid ship's officers of the East India Company's vessels, for example: well-disposed and discreet gentlemen who were only too happy to take charge of a packet for delivery at the end of their run. Even beyond the appeal of a rich reward, however, there is plenty of evidence to show that there prevailed among the majority of chivalrous Englishmen of the time a furtive but mounting sympathy for the caged Eagle, the indomitable fighter who had almost held the world in the grasp of his hand—with every sword pointed at his breast the while, and every villain ready to betray him. Quite obviously the names of these couriers could not usually be recorded, but there is an interesting account of at least one such in Count Bertrand's coded *Cahiers de Sainte Hélène*.

This intriguing passage has to do with the assistance provided by Captain Hamilton of the frigate *Havannah*, a ship of the St. Helena squadron about to depart for England, in the delivery of an

THE FURY FADES

important letter or a packet of such. First there had been a refusal, as was to have been expected, for to undertake such a task was for the captain tantamount to taking his career and commission in his hands. However, the refusal was followed by an overnight visit in Jamestown by the fascinating Madame Bertrand—and the next day that Marshal's dinner table was graced by the presence of the dashing captain himself. When on the day following the *Havannah* set sail, the general entered in his diary, under date of April 21, 1816, the fact of the dinner, adding tersely, *Paquet remis!* It should be noted that only six months had passed for the French on St. Helena, and already the private mail service was operating efficiently—even piquantly.

In similar fashion the script of the famous *Letters from the Cape* was sent out, to be published simultaneously in England and France—as was Napoleon's *Observations on Lord Bathurst's Speech,* as well as much other controversial material designed principally to keep the absent Emperor's memory alive in the minds of both friends and foes. In spite of the fact that enormous damage would have been done to the careers of the many individuals involved in the transmission of these papers, had their identity ever been revealed, there seems never to have been a lack of volunteers. There are strong indications that Captain Dillon of the *Phaeton* was involved—as may well have been the case since he was related to Fanny Dillon, Madame Bertrand herself. Dr. Warden of the *Northumberland* and Dr. Stokoe of the *Conqueror* were almost certainly participants in the scheme to evade British censorship—so that it is possible to conclude that not only were the East India Company's employees willingly involved in this irregular service, but the officers of the fleet as well. And then there were certain influential residents of the island itself who stood ready to lend a kindly hand.

Of these latter the one most strongly suspected by Lowe of being

WHO LIES HERE?

implicated was William Balcombe, the local purveyor and agent of the East India Company—the owner of the pleasant cottage called The Briars, where Napoleon had lodged during the first two months of his exile while Longwood was being prepared for him. He never knew it, but some years before Napoleon's occupancy there had lodged there also the future conqueror of Waterloo, who paused on St. Helena a few days to break the monotony of the long voyage from India. First Wellington then the ex-Emperor of the French, each drawn by his inscrutable fate to that remote place —to the same little room, even, on that unlikely rock at world's end. A supernal playwright, evidently, has no aversion to wild coincidences in his script!

Since this William Balcombe had, by the nature of his duties and function, unlimited opportunity for contact with the officers of every ship that entered Jamestown harbor, and at the same time freedom to come and go in the French quarters, where he attended to the supplies and consumable stores, there can be but little doubt that he carried out many such friendly offices for Longwood as began to occasion the governor uneasy concern about his activities. A considerable degree of esteem was expressed by Napoleon for the sturdy and likable Balcombe and his family, who in turn responded with affectionate regard and many a kindly gesture and act of friendship toward the French.

To sum up, any attempt to identify all the individuals involved in delivering Napoleon's correspondence to Europe and elsewhere, as well as that coming to him from all the world, would be fruitless—for doubtless their name was Legion. The situation was well defined by Admiral Malcolm, commander of the fleet, in a despairing comment to Sir Hudson relative to putting a stop to these illicit goings-on, of which they were frustratedly well aware by then: "We should have to get rid of all the Company's ships, because all their officers are for Napoleon!" Since this situation had

THE FURY FADES

become common knowledge in St. Helena, there is little need to marvel that the unhappy governor could not sleep!

A goodly portion of his proof of Napoleon's success in bypassing the restrictions lay in the series of French and English newspapers forwarded to him from London by an irate Bathurst—the fat articles or lengthy letters from his prisoner up on the hill all inked about by the pen of the indignant minister. Naturally the newspapers were only too happy to print all this matter from so famous a source—it offered the press such a fine chance to twist the government's tail, while at the same time improving circulation. The average Briton, inherently a well-disposed man, was beginning to feel a certain degree of dissatisfaction over the harsh treatment accorded the great man who had, it appeared, chosen to entrust his safety to them rather than to any of the Continental powers—or even to America.

We know then, for a certainty, that Napoleon and his officers had established an eminently successful two-way system of communication with the outside world as early as the middle of 1816. We know that he had, locally and in Europe, more than ample money and credit. We know that both in Europe and the Americas he had hordes of faithful, even fanatical followers, with influential and famous figures to guide and organize their enthusiasm. Of these last there was Madame Mère and beautiful sister Pauline in Italy and ex-King Joseph in America—all independently wealthy and ready to spend their money when called on to support any promising scheme of rescue of the unfortunate son and brother who had so freely lavished wealth and titles on them all in his time of glory. Thus, the preliminaries for launching the Emperor's plan of escape seem to have been completed at an early date, and we may note with admiration what had been accomplished by a prisoner under the closest of military supervision, guarded by regiments of

WHO LIES HERE?

armed soldiers and signalers, supervised by Sir Thomas Reade's net of spies and informers; the object of endless harassments and restrictions, granted only the barest minimum of unsupervised movement, forbidden to hold private speech with any of the island's residents.

In spite of all, and beyond the system of communications described, there were the friendly relations established with a surprising number of local residents and functionaries, the cooperation obtained from many private individuals and merchants —from wealthier individuals down to the slaves at the bottom. The unassailable procedures of the Court barred the palace to any unwelcome visitor—and permanently to the governor. There had been set up, too, a rude system of counterespionage under the Corsican Cipriani, an old hand at the business, which was ever a rich mine of information for the consideration of the agile mind presumably sealed up safely on the foggy crest of Longwood plain. All this was done, and more yet: From that unpleasant aerie where he was lodged, the caged Eagle was able to foil most of Sir Hudson's attacks and, in the manner of the jujitsu expert, to turn them back against the governor in turn—as it were, utilizing the governor's weight to undo him. And undo him he surely did, by means of his writings and the campaigns mounted by his messengers. Napoleon was not one to forgive the many unnecessary humiliations and the base vindictiveness of his jailer. When the latter returned to England, his task completed, he found himself a ruined man—promotion and even pension blocked, ostracized at his club, and the victim of Dr. O'Meara's defamatory charges in the book all Europe was discussing—the *Voice from St. Helena*—wherein Lowe's conduct toward his prisoner was set forth in richly libelous detail. Perhaps the book was libelous—but when Lowe wished to sue the author, counselors dissuaded him, realizing that with the English public opinion as inflamed against him

THE FURY FADES

as it was, he had no hope of winning. He was to die poor and in obscurity.

A strange circumstance is worthy of mention here: Although Lowe's interment in St. Mark's Church, North Audley Street, London, is entered in the parish register—the tomb and marker have vanished, none knows whither or when. It seems an incredible circumstance, but such is the recorded fact. It would appear that Lowe's accounting for his misdeeds, both in his latter days and posthumously, was a severe one indeed. There can be little doubt but that his oblivion was in great part brought about by the government's (and the Prince Regent's) earnest desire to shift the blame and reproach for Napoleon's treatment from their own shoulders to the back of their unimaginative servant—and in this they were immediately successful, of course, since a solitary man makes a much more satisfactory scapegoat than does a cabinet. Napoleon and his agents had already done most of the work for them into the bargain—and poor Lowe was such an easy man to dislike that he seemed to have been designed especially by the Fates for such a sacrifice.

During all this time, elsewhere in the world beyond the waters, loyal hearts and hands had never ceased from their preoccupation with the business of plotting and planning for the release of the absent Emperor. The principal center of this activity was the city of Rio de Janeiro.

The long-dead volcano that is St. Helena lies sixteen degrees south of the equator, well in the path of the southeast trade winds that blow around the world forever. Africa is more than a thousand miles to the east, Brazil eighteen hundred to the west. Since Africa at the time presented but a sterile and fever-ridden coastline, Rio in the west was the only city of consequence proximate to Jamestown. South Africa was of course British, therefore Capetown was

WHO LIES HERE?

out of the question as a base for French plotters. It was not long after Napoleon's exile commenced that Rio became famous for being a focus of most of the plots, as well as the several actual attempts, to abduct or liberate the prisoner. From early in 1816 right through to the report of the Emperor's death in 1821 no year passed without the disclosure of at least one such expedition having been either nipped in the bud or otherwise brought to naught.

The thing to be kept in mind is that hope was never dead, either in Longwood or in the world of Napoleonic sympathizers—never, at any time; freedom and liberation for the Emperor was the theme of an entire way of life for a huge body of enthusiasts and their financial backers. It was tangible, a pervading force, and it was never quenched in spite of thwartings, until the grim news announcing the Emperor's death. And at Longwood, as we have seen, the same spirit was sweeping obstacles aside to effect a similar end.

Detailed summaries of these schemes, as fast as they were brought to light, were forwarded promptly by Lord Bathurst to Plantation House—to the great detriment of Sir Hudson Lowe's blood pressure. Such communications were invariably accompanied by adjurations and counsels of closer restraints for Longwood's people, and these the overwrought governor always carried out to the letter—seeming at times to have derived a savage joy from thus further humiliating and infuriating his captives. The very thought of a well-conceived plot for effecting Napoleon's escape at once threw Lord Bathurst's office into flurries of energetic correspondence, which in turn would send the palsied governor galloping off to Longwood once more—there to prowl and peer disconsolately about the primitive structure so effectively sealed against him. These were the times when the hapless orderly officer was bullied and prodded to provide his daily sightings, so that more than one of them recorded his belief in the permanent

THE FURY FADES

ruination of his health, undermined by the strain and futility of ceaseless patrol in cold and darkness and drenching rain.

A complete description of all these rescue attempts—either planned or actually undertaken—is not required here, although the accounts are extremely interesting. They tend, however, to become hopelessly involved and in many instances appear to have been ineptly conceived. It should be kept in mind, however, that we are looking at these histories with hindsight and are well aware of their futility. The ministers of the British Crown, on the other hand, could not possibly guess all that was in the wind, nor how great might be the threat next to be presented against them and the safe custody of Europe's prisoner—an awesome responsibility that was with them night and day. The certain knowledge that revolutionary parties backed by people of wealth and power were active in the United States, Mexico and South America, and that Napoleon's reappearance in almost any of these areas would (since the latter countries were in the midst of their struggles to cast off the yoke of Spain) act as a spark in a powder keg—these things, and kindred instabilities in Europe, with floods of unendurable poverty rising at home, were but a part of the stern anxieties that English statesmen carried always with them. Hence, the concern implicit in Lord Bathurst's admonitions to Lowe, surging to a high point whenever the report of a new liberating scheme reached him. He could not but early note that the most seriously conceived of these invariably originated in the Americas, and always the concentration point was Rio.

Mexico's revolutionary party sent a delegation to Bordentown, New Jersey, offering the throne of Mexico to Napoleon's brother Joseph, whose natural acquisitiveness had rendered him immensely wealthy during his brief reign as king of Spain. There can hardly remain a doubt but that he was actively or financially involved, more than once, in plots to liberate his famous brother.

WHO LIES HERE?

The insurrectionary activities in both Mexico and South American countries were linked, in the mind of the French ambassador at Washington, with at least one of the major schemes directed against the British guardians of St. Helena. At any rate this minister, the Baron Hyde de Neuville, kept the diplomatic pouches to his home ministers in both Paris and London well charged with detailed and tremendously involved accounts of curious matters transpiring in Washington, Philadelphia and Annapolis—and above all in the celebrated *Champ d'Asile* established by the Bonapartists in Texas.

Today, when one attempts to make a coherent analysis of these accounts, the mind almost immediately becomes bogged down in the incredibly involved windings and turnings devised by men whose methods seem utterly at variance with his own. There are continual comings and goings as new names are introduced, personalities appear and vanish—some of these with apparently crucial roles to manage or with vital tasks to undertake —inevitably one's attention begins to drift away from the confused and apparently directionless pictures presented. Little wonder that these plans came so soon to light and that the principals were so promptly seized and deported or placed under strict surveillance, for every new member of the top-heavy cast became yet another weak link in a chain whose twists and windings and splicings were already a weakness profoundly discouraging, one would have thought.

In Rio, Pernambuco and Buenos Aires both French and British government agents worked closely together, pooling their information and keeping their departments informed of bizarre developments as they were unearthed on the spot. One of the earliest practical results of this collaboration was the seizure by a British naval squadron under Sir Pultenay Malcolm of the tiny island of Ascension lying seven hundred miles to the northwest of St.

THE FURY FADES

Helena. This was done to forestall its capture by a well-known American privateer, the *True-Blooded Yankee,* reported as sailing from Bahia, Brazil. Her crew, so ran the report, had openly declared that they were embarking on a voyage aimed at the release of Napoleon, with their base of operations to be established on Ascension—then uninhabited. This alarming message was relayed to Jamestown by Bathurst's letter of May 14, 1816, whereupon Admiral Malcolm promptly seized and occupied the island. Sure enough—not long afterward a vessel described as "a very fast sailer," consistently outrunning the British frigates sent out to intercept her, appeared in St. Helena waters. Day after day she returned, beating on-and-off as she scouted the island's defenses and continuing to elude the slower warships while adding to the degeneration of Hudson Lowe's nervous system.

The letters of the governor to London reporting this insolent presence still convey a sense of his perturbation and apprehension. Eventually the *True-Blooded Yankee* gave up and was seen no more in the south Atlantic, but she was not the last American ship observed hovering off the forbidden area despite Britain's strict prohibition of these waters to all unauthorized sea traffic. However, with Ascension—and later Tristan da Cunha—occupied by the British there was little that a light sailing craft could effect on her own: She had to have a source of drinking water, and the nearest available to her was back at Rio.

It is of some interest to note that the island of Tristan da Cunha is inhabited today by the descendents of some soldiers of the garrison who elected to stay after the regiments were sent home in 1821—these were augmented from time to time by deserters and women brought from the Cape. Ascension island was maintained under admiralty rule until 1922, when it was joined to the St. Helena administration. Until that time, however, it had lost its identity as an island—since the admiralty does not deal in

WHO LIES HERE?

colonies—and was therefore regarded as a ship; those born there were looked on as having been born at sea, and were registered in the parish of Wapping, London.

This then, the earliest evidence of an organized attempt to free Napoleon, was announced only seven months after his arrival in St. Helena. His friends were losing no time, nor were they then or later sparing of money in mounting their expeditions.

One of the more appealing of the stories of these ever-loyal friends and their hopeful efforts brings up a name more properly—or improperly—belonging to the earlier years of the Emperor's career: one which enthusiasts of the Legend rejoiced to hear spoken again. It was that of the once-beautiful and gallant Pauline Fourès, with whom the young general, far from Paris and his faithless Josephine, became smitten shortly after the taking of Cairo in the Egyptian campaign of 1798. Mme. Fourès had come out with the French forces, contrary to the regulations forbidding wives to accompany their husbands on the expedition. She and a good many other determined young ladies had had their names inscribed on the regimental rolls by grace of the farsighted officers sponsoring them and thereafter did their very best to cram their unmilitary charms into the skintight uniforms of the period. At the same time that verified reports of Josephine's infidelities were filtering through the British Mediterranean patrols to appal and infuriate young General Bonaparte, so did his enraptured gaze light on the lush vision of Lieutenant Fourès' wife in her overstrained hussar costume. Here, he perceived, was that very balm his chafed spirit so sorely required! Like King David in similar affliction, he at once had the deluded young officer transferred —not into "the forefront of the battle" like poor Uriah, but back to France carrying unimportant dispatches.

Thereafter Pauline became luxuriously installed, riding out with Napoleon daily to the cheers and intense appreciation of the

THE FURY FADES

Army—who themselves had to make do with Arab or Ethiopian substitutes, all that was available to them. Pauline was adored by every one of the French soldiers, to whom she became known as Cleopatra, and more familiarly as Belilote. She was ever to be remembered for her high spirits and her kindness.

Although Napoleon throughout his life expressed a certain cynicism in regard to the depth of the emotions of companions of this passing nature, his actual practice toward them continued to be generous and protective always—with a regard and an affectionate loyalty seemingly undiminished by the passage of years. When Belilote managed at last to get herself back to Paris, she found her friend had become too great to be able to encourage her presence at the Tuileries or thus openly defy the jealous Josephine; but he saw to it that she received a home of her own and a pension—for the lieutenant, of course, had been obliged to seek a divorce long before. Still later, under the Empire, a wealthy old husband was found for her so that she was known thereafter as Madame de Ranchoup—continuing to reign as a source of charm and delight to all who knew her.

It seemed that little Belilote had clung to the memory of her Egyptian idyll all her life. When the Empire went down into final disaster, she would have no dealings with those who succeeded it; she set out promptly, leaving all behind her (including Monsieur de Ranchoup) and in 1816 turned up in Rio, accompanied by an officer of the Imperial Guard. It was she, there is reason to believe, who financed the expedition of the *True-Blooded Yankee*—but that failure had not discouraged her. She is known to have thereafter expended every sou of her fortune in backing ventures and schemes directed against St. Helena and the enemies of her Emperor. Another of her associates in Rio was Dick van Hogendorf, one of Napoleon's aides-de-camp at Waterloo and ex-Minister of War in Holland. After that her name appears no more. One may properly

WHO LIES HERE?

pass lightly over these events in the later career of *la petite Belilote,* reflecting that eighteen years had passed since she had first won the regard of the gaunt and brooding young general in those brave early days, and she had not forgotten.

The *Champ d'Asile* was the romantic name given by a number of French expatriates to a celebrated colony they founded in Texas under the leadership of the dashing General Lallemand of Waterloo fame. A schooner named the *Huntress*, chartered and captained by a General Rigaud in the winter of 1817, left Philadelphia laden with cannon, muskets and powder, and after suffering incredible misfortunes sailed up the Trinity River to the site already selected by General Lallemand for the settlement. Invaluable assistance in this undertaking was provided by none other than the notorious pirate Lafitte and his buccaneers. The more than four hundred men and women, entirely unprepared for the countless hardships of their new environment, were to experience every possible reverse and calamity.

The proclaimed object of this colony was the peaceful pursuit of agriculture and the development of a home safe from the vicissitudes of war or the vengeance of Bourbon agents—for in France most of these famous soldiers of the Empire were under proscription or outlawed. But rarely indeed could a more unlikely collection of agriculturalists than these have been gathered together to confront so stern a wilderness! Their minds yet lingered on the paths of glory so recently frequented; around communal campfires they sang their songs of old campaigns, reviving old memories. It appears well established that their leaders were soon in communication with the revolutionists in Mexico—their objective, the supplying of French military aid in the overthrowing of Spain; beyond that none seems to have visioned clearly, or at least specifically.

Rumors of these matters came at last to the ears of President

THE FURY FADES

Monroe, together with a tale of a fantastic plot to free Napoleon and to place him on the Mexican throne. All that was actually contemplated can never be known now, for such things are obviously unlikely to have been set down in the form of incriminating documents. However, the twin dreams of liberating the Emperor and offering his ascent to the Mexican throne as a *fait accompli* had sufficient substance to impress the Spanish governor of San Antonio, for he set forth, at last, with an armed expedition against the *Champ d'Asile*—and the final result was the ruin and dispersal of the colony.

In retrospect it appears grotesque that such world-famous names as those of Marshal Grouchy, Generals Lefèbvre-Desnouettes, Lallemand, Vandamme, Gérard and many another of like vintage should have been regarded as the innocent leaders of a peaceful emigrant group of would-be farmers, all forgetful of their distinguished careers and warlike exploits. A conversation that took place in later years between General Bertrand and Count Metternich included references by the former Grand Marshal to the dates on which the French at Longwood first heard of certain activities of the people at *Champ d'Asile* and their excitement at the possible implications for themselves. A consideration of the entries in the diaries on these dates shows that they are charged with a high excitement not discernible in the rest of the matter, and strongly suggests that Longwood was in close touch with the principals of the Texan colony.

Still in the same connection, news of the most serious enterprise yet undertaken was brought to the attention of the Marquis de Montchenu, the French commissioner on St. Helena, in early 1818, details having been sent him by the French *chargé d'affaires* in Rio. Details of similar dispatches received by the governor and his admiral at once spread through the island's grapevine, throwing the entire island into a fever of speculation. At Longwood,

WHO LIES HERE?

Gourgaud tells us, the excitement was unrestrained as each new rumor was brought through the sentries: Brother Joseph, it was said, was already on the throne of Mexico, and General Clauzel was raising a large infantry force—no doubt for the purpose of assailing the island! All this uproar was occasioned by reports of a combination entered into by three redoubtable champions—at least one being the most unlikely conceivable.

Best known of the three, at least to the French, was General Brayer, a Count of the Empire and a divisional commander at Waterloo, whose flight after that battle had taken him first to the US and then to Buenos Aires—that alluring coast! Another was a Colonel Latapie who, with thirty-two other veteran officers, was directing himself toward Pernambuco, Brazil. The third and most incredible member of the trio was a famous British admiral, one of that spirited and superbly trained group of naval officers deriving from the Nelsonian period, and a great harrier of the French in former years. He was Admiral Lord Cochrane, the future Earl of Dundonald. From his seat in Parliament he had attacked the government of Lord Liverpool and soon after—whether as a result of this indiscretion or not cannot be ascertained—was cashiered, tried, fined and imprisoned on some apparently trumped-up charges of fraud. Driven to an extreme of frenzy by such treatment from a country he had served so well, he promptly turned renegade and offered his sword and services to his former enemies —naturally enough, in Brazil, where the action seemed to be imminent.

The French premier, the Duc de Richelieu, received an exposé of the entire proceedings from his minister in Rio. Lord Cochrane was to supply and man a cruiser of seventy-four tons (in some accounts it was stated to be a "seventy-four"—a much more impressive matter!); the others were bringing "two armed schooners of three hundred tons"—presumably *in toto*—manned by

THE FURY FADES

eighty French officers and seven hundred men from the United States. Here, without doubt, is the point of intersection between this expedition and that devised at the *Champ d'Asile,* for the Texas colony was the only place in the United States that could possibly have supplied so many French, and soldiers at that.

This argosy planned on storming the island fortress with their little fleet, setting a party ashore to seize Napoleon, then returning to Brazil. They had already, according to the French investigators, succeeded in establishing contacts on St. Helena months earlier. The account is here kept simple for brevity's sake, but the much more detailed official account is a matter of record, unbelievable as it may sound. It is not to be wondered at, in view of all the constant and menacing activity, that Sir Hudson Lowe and his superiors in London were drawn into excesses of severity in the restriction and supervision of their dynamic charge. They were well justified in their apprehensions, above all, of what a liberated Napoleon might achieve in the widespread turbulence of the world's political atmosphere—for at this period he was described by many reliable visitors and spectators, as well as by his companions, as being quite as energetic and vigorous both physically and mentally as when he had been at the head of the great empire he had created. The trauma and shock following his crushing defeat at Waterloo had dissipated itself and his driving mind was again beating itself furiously against the bars, reaching outward to all eventualities.

The Brayer-Latapie-Cochrane effort fizzled out like all the others, arriving at its premature doom in the fall of 1817 through the arrest of Latapie in Pernambuco just after he had been set down there by an American schooner. A vigorous examination resulted in his prompt acknowledgment of complicity in the St. Helena plot, and he was sent to Lisbon to be confined there until the French government made up its mind about his fate. General Brayer's cooperation was thus forestalled, and he was thereafter

WHO LIES HERE?

kept under close scrutiny in Buenos Aires. Lord Cochrane then entered the naval services of first Brazil, then Chile, in their respective revolts against Portugal and Spain; later he was to be forgiven at home and his rank in the Navy restored to him. It is worth noting that Napoleon, in his will, left a substantial legacy to General Brayer.

The last of the more notable escape plots of record was initiated by the then Mayor of New Orleans, Nicholas Girod, who with the aid of a circle of wealthy sympathizers set about the task of freeing Napoleon. They built an especially swift schooner, the *Seraphine,* as well as a fine home for their hero's prospective occupancy—the house still stands at the corner of Chartres and St. Louis streets, and is said to be in excellent condition. Alas, just as the *Seraphine* was preparing to sail, the stunning news arrived in New Orleans: *Napoléon est mort!* So the miserable Lowe was to be spared the apprehension of this final threat—although the Longwood people had been kept well abreast of the progress in the *Seraphine*'s construction, noting it with keen interest although they by that time were well aware that the life of the principal prisoner was fast fading. In later years Count Bertrand, accompanied by Marshal Ney's eldest son, paid a visit to New Orleans and told the citizens of the pleasure that Girod's efforts had occasioned at Longwood; he presented the city with a marble bust of Napoleon to further commemorate the venture and their so amply manifested goodwill.

The story of these abortive schemes and expeditions—only a fraction of those on record—is here set forth to demonstrate how, during the entire St. Helena captivity, scores and hundreds of resolute men, men of proven courage and many of them wealthy as well, not only occupied themselves in devising bold schemes for setting their Emperor free, but actually got many of them under way—even going so far in more than one instance as to confront

THE FURY FADES

the supreme sea power of the age in the very waters of the forbidden island. The attitude was definitely *not* one of lassitude or despair—either in the world at large or within the walls of Longwood itself: most particularly not there!

All these accounts are, of course, matters of official record and admit of no dispute. On the contrary they strongly suggest, in a few instances, that even greater names—names of power and wealth—may well have been involved or had contributed privately a share of their fortunes. When, after May of 1821, the French were permitted to leave St. Helena, both Montholon and Bertrand stated that they enclosed certain private papers in glass jars and buried them by night in Longwood's grounds—to forestall the anticipated search of their baggage, which was in fact carried out at the governor's orders prior to their embarkation. It does not seem that there was any opportunity then, nor again during the return visit made by the French expedition of 1840, to recover these containers: The French officers were, even then, under a certain degree of scrutiny, their movements noted and commented upon. No doubt they realized it was as yet too soon for such revelations as these so carefully concealed documents must have dealt with; times were not yet ripe for Bonapartist causes, and at all events the papers were secure enough where they were. Attempts are still made, from time to time, to locate these buried bottles; some day, inevitably, they will be stumbled upon, and then what strange facts may come to the light of day after so many years of darkness!

Part Two
EXITS AND AN ENTRANCE

Wherever wood can swim, there I am sure to find this flag of England!

—N<small>APOLEON</small>

I, serving as a captain of a legion of Rome, have learned and pondered this thought: in life there are two pursuits, love and power. No man can have both.

—inscription found in the Libyan desert

THERE IS a weary piece of nonsense reiterated by earnest but thoughtless souls, regarding Napoleon's Longwood domicile as made known to them through the standard biographies. It runs like this, with many variations: "But how can you *possibly* maintain that there was anything unknown or even unsuspected about Napoleon's life during those years? Surely never in history was one man so *closely watched,* so securely guarded day and night—never for a moment without an observor, a spy, sentries galore and men stationed on every adjacent hilltop! Why, every moment, almost, of his day and night were accounted for. . . !" And so on. This meaningless rubbish even finds its way into recent discussions, written by responsible types who wouldn't dream in their ordinary pursuits of buying a secondhand car on the sort of testimony they are depending on to support this hoary illusion.

It would be best to get this naïve concept out of the way at once, showing that far from being true in any part the exact opposite is more nearly consistent with the facts of the case.

First, regarding the accounts we possess telling of the life within Longwood's dreary walls—this "moment by moment" retailing of each day's and each night's goings-on—what are they, who wrote them? Why, who *could* write them except the French officers who lived with Napoleon, since no one else was admitted without

WHO LIES HERE?

ceremony and protocol to the interior of Napoleon's home? All, absolutely all, we know is obtained from the memoirs of the four French "courtiers"—Bertrand, Montholon, Las Cases and Gourgaud, and that of Marchand, the Emperor's valet and close friend. There came later brief reminiscences by one Ali, a servant, and by the last arrival, Dr. Antommarchi. These last were frankly written for money and add nothing to the story—indeed they have to be heavily discounted since they are largely out of agreement with the principal, and responsible, accounts. Of the memoirs, those of the Count de Las Cases could tell only of the period up to the end of 1816, when he was deported, and so his journal covers but the first thirteen months. Gourgaud's account, regarded as very trustworthy, ends with the year 1817, when he left. Thus, there are only three testimonies from inside the walls that are eyewitness accounts right up to 1821 and the end—and of these, Count Bertrand's is episodic and sometimes secondhand, because he lived some distance away, at Hutt's Gate.

The reports offered by the British were collections of gossip, spies' retailings and reports of their observations taken through telescopes, Hudson Lowe's bales of official correspondence—and the orderly officer's terse and increasingly infrequent accounts of his sightings made from the grounds. No English official was permitted inside the house—all business being conducted through the Grand Marshall at his home—with the exception of extremely rare professional calls by an Army or Navy doctor. Napoleon's first physician, the Irishman O'Meara, wrote his important *Voice from St. Helena* specifically to denounce Lowe's treatment of his prisoner, not to gossip about whatever he had seen or overheard at Longwood; he was dismissed almost at the end of 1818, and his story stops there also.

There are the reports of some of Napoleon's distinguished visitors, usually included in their book of travels as an added

EXITS AND AN ENTRANCE

attraction; and there is the delightful diary of little Betsy Balcombe, the fifteen-year-old daughter of William, the company purveyer of the East India Company. From the very beginning Betsy had been a source of joyous companionship for the Emperor and she was granted free access to him at almost any hour. But, like O'Meara, the Balcombes felt compelled to leave in 1818; it is evident that the only detailed accounts embracing the entire six-year period are those mentioned above: the memoirs of Bertrand, Montholon and Marchand.

After 1818 there would be just these three to write the story of the prisoner's private life. There would be, from then on, but one visitor permitted in the house. There would be no gallops about the island, under escort or otherwise—no appearance in public: Months on end were to pass when the Longwood tenant would be absolutely invisible, seen by no one—not even by the orderly officer. There exists but one report from the period 1818-21 implying that the speaker had seen Napoleon at close range—and this was by a man in his late seventies and notably senile. Aside from this old chap, no one, no one at all who had seen the Emperor prior to 1818, ever claimed to have laid eyes on him thereafter—on St. Helena, at least.

With the exception, of course, of the French—those who wrote—the only ones who were able to write—our only inside stories of Longwood and its tenant.

What has happened to that fond belief that "no one was ever so closely watched, spied on through every hour of the day and night . . ."?

His figure, after 1818, was only rarely observed *at all,* and only infrequently indeed did someone report sighting, at medium to long range, a short, stoutish man garbed in the well-known uniform and hat, pottering about briefly on the grounds. Ample support for these statements can be found in any of the recognized

WHO LIES HERE?

St. Helena histories. The first procedure might well be to inspect more closely the events of that significant year of 1818, before which all is clear regarding the Napoleonic presence, at least, but after which descends a veil of obscurity that must be thrust aside boldly and with decision if the mystery it has so long and effectively shrouded is to be comprehended. The essential trick is to achieve a clear and unbiased viewpoint—one not preconditioned by vain repetitions of thoughtless catchphrases, but open to the startling clarity of a more truly informed vision.

It is time to inspect more closely the mystery of St. Helena, so often referred to in the literature of the subject, and to try to find answers for the questions that present themselves so insistently.

The brief résumé of the many reported escape plots demonstrates their common futility and impracticality; they were one and all wildly romantic and hopelessly involved schemes doomed to collapse long before they could be well launched—and so they must be dismissed from any serious consideration. As history records, Napoleon knew of the existence of most of these plans for his enlargement and invariably dismissed them from his mind —save to enjoy, no doubt, the flurries of concern their exposure gave his enemies. There was only one plan in which he was interested and that was, as usual, his own. He was of necessity obliged to take his officers into his confidence—their assistance and their cooperation was going to be required for an indefinite period afterward.

It is more than probable that from the very beginning of his term on St. Helena he had been steadily employed in forming the structure and embellishing the matter of his legend—that of which his entire career had been the glorious foundation. His swiftly dictated memoirs, at first entrusted to Las Cases, Gourgaud and O'Meara, formed the gleaming battlements and towers, later augmented by other accounts to be published in their turn by

EXITS AND AN ENTRANCE

Bertrand, Montholon, Marchand, reinforced by the reminiscences of many a famous visitor and tourist passing through prior to 1818. Indeed, once the colossal affair was well begun, every word or minute detail concerning the exile's story could do nothing but add its quota to its interest and fascination for men. Well the Emperor realized all this—as he once observed to Bertrand after an evening of recounting the magic memories, "What a romance my life has been!" One of the greatest of such in all the world's history, of course; what a shame it would have been if its ending had not been well written! But there would be no danger of that—too many enthusiastic pens were setting down that part of the tale that would become the final installment—and that would, as a by-product, render them all wealthy men.

Napoleon was well aware then that his career devoted to garnering glory for France had been the stuff of dreams, of fables; remained the refining, the palliation of excesses, the reasoned accounting for what his foes were naming ruthless ambition and common bloodlust—whereas all his acts had been ideally conceived for the enrichment and exaltation of his people, by the hopes nourished in his heart for the creation of a dynasty fit to offer France—and by his great love for his son, the King of Rome!

Something of all this would get into the story via the enraptured imaginings of his amanuenses; later on the gleaming edifice would be crowned by the record of his stoic martyrdom on the harsh rock lost in the remote seas—Prometheus, who had brought down immortal fire and offered it to the nations but to be betrayed and denounced, then chained down on this volcanic stone while a vulture (in the form of Sir Hudson Lowe) tore incessantly at his liver. Obviously, this part was a *must*—it was the style in which all the magnificent myths of the ancients were concluded.

"If Jesus Christ had not been martyred," he had once observed, "He could never have become the Son of God."

WHO LIES HERE?

Accordingly he conceived that it was requisite that he should first dictate the memoirs—suitably edited and revised, of course—that the world was to receive, then so to live, speak and conduct himself as to provide the appropriate subject matter his observers would note down for inclusion in the noble finale. Beyond that, all that was required of him was that he go on enduring until released by death. By that time all the requisite ingredients would have been manufactured and laid ready for assembly, each in its proper place.

But—he had no intention of waiting there for the release of death. Not by any manner of means!

Life—thwarted but vigorous life—still expressed itself in the Emperor's vital frame and tissues, with all the mental exuberance to be looked for in a man of his age and temperament. In August of 1818 he became forty-nine and was still a young and surprisingly energetic man—a man hardened physically and by no means as overweight as we have been led to believe by certain writers. As he had at first protested to Lowe, he was accustomed to riding "at least twenty miles a day," and felt the need of such exercise as routine. On the subject of his physical condition there is a good deal of the recorded testimony of experienced observers, from the time of his boarding the *Bellerophon* through the first three years of Longwood, and invariably it speaks of their surprise at discovering the Emperor to be in excellent condition and by no means as fleshy as they had been led to imagine him.

When Napoleon came up the side of the British warship that was to bear him to England, Captain Maitland wrote of him in his diary: "A remarkably strong, well-built man, about five foot seven inches in height, his limbs particularly well formed. The teeth were good, no gray hair." Ships' captains were then, as since, shrewd observers of men's physiques.

Again, in June of 1817 the British Ambassador to China, Lord

EXITS AND AN ENTRANCE

Amherst, paused with his party in Jamestown and sought an interview with Napoleon. He then presented himself at Longwood with his staff of nine on July 1. Among his people were the Embassy secretary Henry Ellis, and a Dr. Abel. Lord Amherst was, like all the others, very favorably impressed with the Emperor's appearance and pleasing manner. Henry Ellis wrote of him that ". . . his person was not by any means overgrown, and he appeared in good health." Dr. Abel later wrote that "Bonaparte's person has nothing of that morbid fullness which I had been led to expect. On the contrary, I scarcely recollect to have seen a form more expressive of strength and even of vigor. It is true that he was very large, considering his height of five feet seven inches, but his largeness had nothing of unwieldiness . . . his whole form, indeed, was so closely knit that firmness might be said to be its striking characteristic."

Yet another witness may be quoted in this connection—a Captain Basil Hall of the brig *Alceste,* who visited Longwood on August 13, 1817. He stated: "The Emperor's corpulency, at this time reported to be excessive, was by no means remarkable; he differed considerably from the pictures and busts I had seen of him. His flesh looked, on the contrary, firm and muscular. Not the smallest trace of a wrinkle was discernible, nor an approach to a furrow in any part of his countenance. His health and spirits were excellent."

The heights given by these gentlemen are of interest, since so many people have been convinced that Napoleon was a much shorter man. This misconception may have originated, perhaps, in a confusing report made by Dr. Antommarchi in his report of the Emperor's autopsy. For the time being we can content ourselves with a reference to Napoleon's dossier, made at the time of his graduation from the Military College. He was then just turned sixteen, and his height is given, in metric equivalents, as five feet five and one-half inches. It would seem highly likely that a boy of that age—to be better fed thereafter—might add on another inch or two in the next few years; according to these witnesses and yet others, he had done so.

At all events the foregoing should settle the matter of his physical condition and his zest and enthusiasm for yet more experiencing of whatever life might have in reserve for him. He said of himself that he still had twenty years ahead of him—and what man of his age then could reasonably predict more than this for himself?

He had no intention of dying on St. Helena. His words and actions indicate that from the very beginning he had made up his mind to leave that grim and lonely place, and in so doing to enjoy the last laugh—in secret—over the arrogant English ministers and their fatuous Prince Regent, who had, he considered, grossly betrayed and humiliated him.

Instead, the martyrdom requisite to the fulfillment of his legend would be supplied, quite involuntarily of course, by another. There would be a dead "Emperor" in Longwood some day, even as the British and all the Continent were so impatiently anticipating, and should that one have shown, perhaps, an uncooperative tendency to defer his demise, some one at least among the frustrated exiles might be depended on to accelerate it. That unfortunate's life would be the only barrier separating them from their homes and the resumption of their careers. Then, when at last the momentous news was carried around the world, the kings and ministers releasing their long-pent breath, he—the actual and only Napoleon—happily ensconced in some carefully selected niche of private residence, a place undreamed of by his foes of old—would relax also, knowing that at last he was truly free. No man can be freer than that one whom his foes have formally pronounced dead and buried.

EXITS AND AN ENTRANCE

In brief, Napoleon was planning to have his cake and eat it, too; this was to be the perfection of his method, what stamped it with his peculiar genius.

The unerasable fact of Waterloo still rankled in his broodings; he was never quite able to comprehend how the business had gone so wrong for him. "How I wish I could do it over again!" was a frequent comment made to his companions on the *Northumberland*. So he had lost his touch, had he? His genius had deserted him and all that was left him was an ordinary mind, misled by remembered triumphs? He would show them—and history—that the intellect that had created the victory of Austerlitz, that perfection of military strategy, was still at his service, and his vanishing would be a work of art comparable to it among all recorded and legendary escapes.

First, here is a list of the many departures from the Emperor's household during the significant year of 1818. Then, a discussion of the more impressive, each in turn.

In February the Emperor's trusted majordomo, bodyguard, servant and intelligence agent, Cipriani the Corsican, died after sudden agony with every evidence of having been poisoned.

In March General Gourgaud, a devoted confidant turned malcontent, left for England. The well-loved Balcombe family left ten days later.

Count Las Cases, sent away the previous year under suspicion of holding communication with European confederates, arrived at Frankfurt in January—after deliberate delays on Lowe's part, which held him many months in Cape Town, South Africa.

On June 18 six of Napoleon's servants left for Europe. One could imagine that out of consideration for their futures, they might have been secretly advised to do so. Time was growing short.

WHO LIES HERE?

On August 2 Dr. O'Meara, denounced and discharged by Sir Hudson Lowe, was sent away in disgrace.

On August 22 Count Balmain, the Russian Commissioner on St. Helena, left for a protracted vacation in Rio. The Austrian Commissioner, von Stürmer, left also and returned to his own country without ever having set eyes on the man he had been sent to keep under observation.

Toward the end of this interesting year Madame Bertrand began to bring increasing emotional pressure on her husband with the object of inducing him to leave. Madame Montholon did likewise, and when her husband did not yield to her entreaties, she herself left St. Helena early in the next year.

From that time on only Count Bertrand, with his wife and family, and Count Montholon remained of the privileged companions of Napoleon—and the Bertrands were lodged remote at Hutt's Gate, over a mile distant. After the opening of 1819 then, only Count Montholon and the valet, Marchand, remained of Napoleon's friends in the Longwood house.

There would be only one visitor admitted to the house after the fall of 1818 and until the prisoner's death in May of 1821. One visitor only, and only once, in almost three years. After that no one, with the exception of the two doctors and the senile old man, was ever to see the prisoner again, in life, and under circumstances permitting positive identification.

But—and here one may pick up the persistent chorus still echoing—what of the vaunted detailed, day-by-day account of his life—that existence than which none is more particularized, the focus of the entire island's attention, the *raison d'être* for the whole expensive installation of St. Helena, of Sir Thomas Reade's brutal spy methods, of the huge garrison, the widespread signaling system, the patrolling fleet of warships? How could all those eyes

EXITS AND AN ENTRANCE

have been blinded and their mutually supportive testimony be in error?

Let it be repeated once more, before proceeding to particulars: No orderly officer, no spy-servant or gardener, no soldier or officer of the garrison or fleet, no official, was ever able, after the autumn of 1818, to swear that he had looked on the prisoner at a reasonable range and positively identify him as the famous man they had been sent to this far end of the world to guard and observe. The most any of them would have been able to swear to would have been that they had seen—at rare intervals and from a distance, or briefly through an open window into the gloom beyond, or strolling in the little private garden—a short, plump figure, garbed in the costume then, as now and forever, associated with but one personage out of the entire world. Cocked hat, dark green tunic, white knee breeches—to this day these are all that is required to conjure up the instant identity of the Emperor, for masquerade or stage or screen. They were sufficient then, too—already legendary; a close scrutiny of all the reported sightings of "General Bonaparte" will disclose that this appearance was, in fact, all the gazers had seen—on those increasingly rare occasions when they had seen anything at all—and could attest to.

What then of the testimony of the French—Montholon's, Bertrand's and Marchand's, with a few additions from the "service" section, such as Ali's, eager to get in on the financial rewards in later years? The first three at least are detailed accounts, all in general agreement as to the intimate life of Longwood right up to the final evacuation and return to Europe. If all these were collaborators in a certain grand deception, with a death sentence as possible punishment should their guilt be discovered, would not a common self-interest as well as loyalty to their master dictate the agreed-on matter of the memoirs they were to offer to the world?

WHO LIES HERE?

After they left for France in 1821, Montholon—always in urgent need of funds—nevertheless withheld publication of his book until 1847 when France was under a new regime and in a less vindictive era. Bertrand's coded material was held so long it was finally lost, to be discovered, translated and published in 1959—and Marchand's book was similarly delayed. The reminiscences of the others—Las Cases, Gourgaud and O'Meara—could treat only of periods prior to 1816, 1817 and 1818 respectively, and so are without any bearing on the crucial period. Beyond these, the self-serving story of the pseudo-doctor Antommarchi—*Les Derniers moments de Napoléon*—was withheld from publication until 1825 and was of necessity confined to an account of the last few months—the final period of his patient's increasingly more severe symptoms and eventual demise. It suffers, moreover, from glaring inaccuracies and distortions designed to cast luster on the writer, and it is considered wholly untrustworthy.

Thus, having briefly attempted a new and critical consideration of what has been told of this period, it may be allowed that there could be a great deal wrong with the attitude conventionally adopted regarding the "total vigilance" exercised on Napoleon's "every action." It will be more conclusively shown that from 1818 on, at least, the phrases have little significance or value.

The departures of 1818 have been listed first because of their impressive number, and again because in no other year did even a small fraction of this total defect from the Longwood *ménage*: a thing suggestive in itself.

Las Cases arrived in Europe in January, although his departure had taken place much earlier; nevertheless, as the first of the "intimate" group about Napoleon to leave St. Helena, his story should come first in the series.

Like all the others who had volunteered to accompany the exiled Emperor, he was under proscription in France, and he was not to

EXITS AND AN ENTRANCE

be permitted to land in either England or Holland. His old contacts, however, were still available to him, and through these he at once set about mounting a vigorous publicity campaign on behalf of his recent master. Marie Louise, the Russian Emperor as well as that of Austria, the Bonaparte brothers and sisters, Prince Metternich of Austria and Lord Liverpool in England—all these and others were individually addressed and adjured, in the name of compassion and historical perspective, to intervene on behalf of the great figure so miserably persecuted and destroyed. In his letters there was nothing the little man overlooked or forgot, nothing conceivable in the way of persuasion left unemployed.

The story of the removal of Las Cases from St. Helena is charged with minor mysteries and ambiguities. First of all it is apparent that a technique was employed which, a little later, was refined and again utilized to get General Gourgaud out: tales of jealousies and intolerable resentments, of "bad blood" and of acrimonious debates between the Longwood people were permitted to emanate from their quarters for several months before a final action or an outright rupture took place. The attempts at spy work within the French domicile, ordinarily fruitless, became of a sudden unusually successful and reports were sent to Plantation House on even the most trivial conduct within hours of its occurrence—as Napoleon was certainly well aware. Hudson Lowe was advised that Las Cases had from the beginning earned the envy and hatred of his compatriots, because of his rather unctuous deference to the Emperor's whims and to the fact that his company and conversation appeared to have become more pleasing to his master than that of any of the others; in such crowded quarters his position had become so nearly insupportable that he was ripe to apply to the governor for permission to return to Europe. Longwood, moreover, was making doubly sure of attaining its objective and appears to have worked out yet another plan for bringing it to pass.

WHO LIES HERE?

Las Cases commenced by writing a bold letter to the Baroness von Stürmer, the wife of the Austrian commissioner on St. Helena, protesting to her concerning the arduous conditions of his master's exile; no one could know better than he that such conduct as this was forbidden and that the recipient was obliged to forward the communication to the governor instantly. Similarly he proceeded to write in the same vein to several of the senior British officers; shortly afterward Lowe wrote Lord Bathurst to the effect that although everyone at Longwood was diligent in breaking regulations and in abusing his tolerance and liberality, Las Cases was the most incorrigible of all—and he requested permission for the deportation of the count. This denunciation, in view of the mildness, courtesy and inoffensiveness of that diminutive Imperial Secretary, was an almost ludicrous overstatement—save that Las Cases had deliberately rendered himself liable to its application.

Shortly he appeared to fall into a most obvious trap, neatly prepared for him by the ingenious governor. His onetime servant, a slave named James Scott, rather too persistently volunteered to deliver letters in London for him, as Sir Hudson (or so he stated) had found employment for him with an unnamed person who was shortly leaving for London. Needless to relate, the slave was "captured" and incriminating messages that had been entrusted to him by Las Cases were discovered sewn under the lining of his coat. The count was at once seized by Sir Thomas Reade in person and taken away, in full view of Napoleon, to be lodged in a distant cottage and there held incommunicado. It cannot be denied that he had deliberately and energetically invited this treatment—both in the writing of his improper letters and in accepting the slave's too timely proposal, which even an amateur would have known at once was a trap of the most apparent variety. One cannot help but feel, also, that Napoleon was party to his secretary's indiscretions, for all these things could hardly have been contemplated and

EXITS AND AN ENTRANCE

carried out without his promptings, or at least his cognizance. An interesting fact emerges from the testimony of this James Scott, as sworn to Hudson Lowe in the proceedings against Las Cases. He established that on that particular evening of November, 1816, he had had to return to Longwood repeatedly in order to be admitted to the count, and had penetrated the ring of sentries (at night drawn together almost closely enough to touch one another) no fewer than six times, without detection! That must have opened Lowe's eyes wide with horror as he contemplated the deficiencies of his guard system. Young Betsy Balcombe has also recorded the ease with which she was able to pass through the sentries, whenever she wished to make an unannounced visit to her comrade, the Emperor. These facts may be kept in mind when it is time to consider the problem of Napoleon himself effecting such a penetration, if the need for it ever presented itself to him.

But as to the fate of Las Cases, there followed almost a comedy of cross-purposes. Lowe, beginning rather to like the inoffensive little count on closer acquaintance, and perceiving moreover a splendid opportunity for reintroducing a controllable factor of his own in the disturbed and intriguing atmosphere of Longwood, made the friendliest overtures, finally offering to send the count back and to smooth matters over for him there. But of course this was by no means what was wanted—What! After all this trouble to arrange the thing? No, the ex-secretary wrote sadly, no; it was all too late, the damage done. He had been humbled and shamed in the Emperor's actual presence by Reade's rough arrest, effected on Longwood's very lawn; he would always be an object of reproach, of pity, in Napoleon's mind. That he could never endure. Only if his master should *order* him to return, of course—and so on. Whereupon the latter, through Count Bertrand, expressed himself as so indifferent to the outcome, and both sides played their roles with such precision (although they had no possibility of com-

WHO LIES HERE?

municating directly with each other) that Lowe was left no choice as to his procedures and the Las Cases, father and son, were duly installed on the *Griffin* sloop of war and sent off—the long way, that of the Cape. It seems probable that Lowe may have smelt an odor of rat, for at his orders they were held eight months more, in a sort of quarantine process, before being permitted to sail from Capetown for Europe. Thus, the count's energetic program on behalf of his master was delayed until the last days of 1817, no doubt to the helpless fury of himself and his late companions.

The first piece had been played, though probably not to its best effect, and was in position nevertheless for the opening of the campaign of 1818.

The performance had been without any doubt most instructive to the conspirators: a good rehearsal. Reade's spy work had shown them that by dropping their guard they could at any time achieve instant contact with the governor—for the installation of any idea or belief they wished implanted in that worthy's consciousness. They had learned, above all, that even as innocuous a man as was Las Cases, and as unimpeachably of the *noblesse* and *émigré* class into the bargain—the English had yet found him unacceptable and had refused him permission to land in their country; France the same. Troublesome! It would be necessary to build up the next candidate much more carefully: After all, the enemy had been aware, and Las Cases had never denied it, that he was utterly devoted to Napoleon. How about sending someone who had learned, say, to hate and abominate the Emperor, one who would eagerly contrive any harm, utter any calumny against him, appear willing and happy to cause him almost any damage?

It would *have* to be such a one, after Las Cases' failure by opposite qualifications to win his country's confidence. It was worth a try; it promised well—and there was literally no other way

EXITS AND AN ENTRANCE

in which a Bonapartist straight from St. Helena could be set down in either England or France. After all, Lowe and the others had *almost* accepted Las Cases toward the end; only his well-recognized adulation of Napoleon had finally militated against him when it came to a matter of permitting him free movement in Europe. To think that Louis XVIII had refused to admit a genuine aristocrat, a scion of one of the really old families—the taint of Bonapartism must be offensive indeed to such royal nostrils, and persistent, too. They hadn't given that part enough consideration, obviously; well, the next applicant was going to be freed from *that* sort of handicap—he would present himself thoroughly purged of error, indisputably cured and forever immune to the hideous Napoleonic incubus.

And on the credit side, beside the experience won, there was this, too: The eloquent voice of Las Cases was to go on, indefatigably, working on men's minds and opinions, tempering old animosities and stirring up new sympathies as old achievements were recalled and honored.

The member of the Emperor's suite selected for the next assault was General Baron Gaspard Gourgaud—thirty-four years of age, an artilleryman with a military record dating back to 1802 and characterized by dash, gasconading, and an almost hysterical devotion to Napoleon. He had been in the retreat from Moscow and claimed to have saved the Emperor's life; at Waterloo he had done well also, and at the last had pleaded with tears for the privilege of sharing the exile. His excessive devotion to his master was naturally well known to the British—a liability. But suppose it were gradually revealed to them that in the long months of enforced proximity to his idol, a radical change in his emotional bias had taken place, that he had at first commenced to display mad fits of jealousy when his master happened to evince an

WHO LIES HERE?

occasional preference for the company of others, and that now he had become increasingly morose and resentful—alternately inflamed with violent resentments or plunged back into moods of black boredom and disgust, or intervals of irrational weeping, somber with regrets!

What if, after some months of this increasingly erratic behavior (every facet of which would, they were assured, be studiously reported to Lord Bathurst by Lowe), the Baron should then begin to evince a more active impatience with his lot, the disillusionment with the Emperor now ripening into disgust and even hatred? That he should then approach Lowe and demand to be sent home, or at least to England, where he could let Bathurst and the Prince Regent know something of the real truth of Longwood, of Napoleon's lies and deceptions and scheming, his artifices and cunning defiance of Lowe's regulations? It would have to be a good act, and it would have to contain enough meat to convince the British of the defector's sincerity—that is to say, he would actually have to betray Napoleon, at least a little, and to reveal some private matters, in particular those of which, they well knew, the British already had cognizance. It would damage the Emperor's prestige to a minor extent—but he was a known schemer anyway, and could afford to laugh at such petty revelations as Gourgaud would make. As for that officer, it would be harder on *his* reputation in the long run, for he would be accused by Bonapartists across the world of treachery and infamy.

It was not in the least difficult for any of the French staff to obtain official permission to leave St. Helena—such defections were rather encouraged: The more that should wish to leave, the less the number of mouths to be fed and the more tractable the prisoner might be expected to become as his prestige and authority were diminished, by no matter how little.

So formal history must of necessity deal quite harshly with poor

EXITS AND AN ENTRANCE

General Gourgaud; he appears in the records as an unstable, pathetically incompetent sort of man—vacillating, boastful, weeping, posturing, morbid. One cannot help but feel that "General Bonaparte" must have experienced considerable relief in at last getting rid of the fellow. However, it might be better if one kept in the forefront of the mind that this was a distinguished professional soldier who, in thirteen years of continuous campaigning, had risen from second lieutenant to brigadier general and baron of the Empire, all under the hawk eye of the great captain himself, to whom he became aide-de-camp. There is yet one other fact regarding the background of this dissimulating officer that could have had some bearing on his quite extraordinary performance of 1818: He was descended from a family of well-known actors.

Relations between Gourgaud and the Emperor appeared to worsen toward the end of 1817, until in the month of February, 1818, there was news of a violent rupture between the two. This scene had taken place in the presence of the Grand Marshal, General Bertrand—which discreet officer could be relied on to see that the account of the deplorable affair was reported to at least one of the several contacts he maintained in Jamestown society. Count Bertrand was regarded, quite properly, as a "safe" man—one conservative and prudent in counsel, not inclined to gossip. His quiet and well-controlled observations—to the English orderly officer, say, or one of the Allied Commissioners, or even, perhaps, with one of Sir Thomas Reade's creatures—never appeared to be indiscreet revelations but more the guarded and thoughtful comments of a seriously concerned official. Madame Bertrand's English has already been described as excellent; because of that, and because she was acknowledged to be the most beautiful and the best-dressed woman on the island, she fascinated the British officers of the garrison and enjoyed a considerable degree of freedom in her movements. (That "packet" that Count Bertrand had noted in his diary as having been delivered to Captain Hamilton of the *Havannah* was neither the first nor the last of such things that this animated and amiable lady found means of forwarding.)

That Longwood had confidently expected that Gourgaud, after his prospective departure, would be permitted to reside in France is indicated by Napoleon's instruction to his emissary recorded in the latter's diary for February 2, 1818: "It will be best for you to say that you are leaving for reasons of health. O'Meara will give you a certificate to that effect . . . once back in France you will best be able to judge what immediate course you should take." What course the Emperor was referring to is not made clear, since according to Gourgaud he left the room at this point without further amplification. There is no reason to think that at this late date any further discussion would have been necessary, and in any event nothing more than this could have been entered in a journal liable to inspection by the British: The general was to set sail for England within a month's time.

Well before then the French had learned of the vigorous campaign that Las Cases had launched on their behalf, barred though he yet was from his native country. Accordingly Gourgaud and his compatriots increased their efforts to impress their captors with the truth of the absolute conversion of the bitterly disillusioned general, with the fact of his long-smoldering loathing for his master. The machinery for effecting his departure was set into motion and Sir Hudson, for nearly a year well apprised of all those bitter scenes so carefully staged for his benefit, up on the hill, cooperated with a gentlemanly solicitude: Gourgaud was promptly delivered from the environment now become so intolerable to him and installed in a cottage that Lowe provided—with a co-tenant named Lieutenant Basil Jackson.

This lieutenant was later to be employed as a spy and informer on Madame Montholon—pushing his concept of duty in that

EXITS AND AN ENTRANCE

quarter to the extent of creating a romantic interlude for that greatly bored lady—and when, early the next year, she departed from St. Helena and took up residence in Brussels, the lieutenant, like spring, was not far behind: Stories of their liaison continued to trickle back to Longwood. She was doubtless expected to continue to provide Reade with choice items of inside material, via Jackson's reports, but it is indeed doubtful if he obtained anything of value by his industry—in the way of information, at least.

At any rate Gourgaud could hardly be other than well aware of his situation with regard to his new companion, and he went about the work of denunciation of his late master with a will, as though free for the first time to express himself without restraint. Whatever the British appeared to show interest in, whatever would most reassure them as to the correctness of their mode of conduct toward the prisoners (for there was a continuous attack from Liberal elements on the government as to the unchivalrous and even cruel conduct, as they charged, exercised against Napoleon)—all this the young general supplied in full measure reinforced by repeated instances.

This material was gratefully received in England by a ministry grown sensitive to this particular phase of political pressure, and all of Gourgaud's items were eagerly considered: Napoleon was faking his illnesses—in reality he was as sound as the pound, and a lot of those symptoms he made so much fuss about dated back at least to Moscow and were of no serious import. He was able to escape at any time he wished to do so, being in communication with powerful friends in many parts of the world. Gourgaud went on to describe to his incredulous auditors a dozen ways in which the Emperor might readily leave his island prison—the "red herring" technique, of course, for they all involved techniques that would have been utterly repugnant to Napoleon's sense of dignity and historical appropriateness.

WHO LIES HERE?

In his enthusiasm for the part—for a good general has ever a touch of the ham in his makeup, and doubtless Gourgaud was reverting somewhat to his ancestral type into the bargain—he no doubt went a bit overboard at times, for Montholon sent him a note stating, "The Emperor, my dear Gourgaud, considers that you are overplaying your role. . . !" This note, so very difficult to account for in the orthodox histories, is unquestioningly in Montholon's handwriting, as acknowledged by the French biographer Paul Frémeaux, who also concedes that the paper's watermark is proper for the earlier St. Helena years. The spy work between Longwood and Plantation House, as can be learned from this incident among many, was a two-way street as well as a rapid one.

That this total performance was successful in deluding his opponents is shown by the fact that the Allied Commissioners agreed among themselves that the general was by far too light-weight a character for Napoleon to have selected him for any secret mission, and that his disaffection was no doubt genuine enough. His change of allegiance did not, however, impress favorably either the French or the Russian commissioner, and in their reports to their governments they were only mildly enthusiastic about the young officer's potential value to the Bourbon cause. That this lack of appreciation had been occasioned by Gourgaud's unrestrained histrionics is probably true, but it is doubtful that even unqualified endorsement could have effected his return to France against the pronounced enmity of the king to all things Bonaparte-tinged, and in particular to French veterans of Waterloo. But at last he was off—entrusting to Count Balmain, the Russian commissioner who accompanied him to the docks, a last-minute salvo of malicious threats against the Emperor. Balmain would see that these were well publicized. This *was* a juicy bit of scandal, in all truth! Gourgaud's arrival in England was impatiently awaited, and when

EXITS AND AN ENTRANCE

in early May the *Campden* deposited the still fulminating aide on Plymouth's shores he was at once whisked to London to be quizzed and grilled in earnest.

That General Gourgaud appears to have deceived the worldly and sophisticated Count Balmain is perhaps the highest testimony to his abilities. Balmain was the only one of the commissioners possessing even a modicum of brain or of background for his career. He was, in fact, an experienced diplomat of excellent lineage and demonstrable intelligence. In one of his periodic reports, which were invariably and avidly read by the Czar himself, he recounted Gourgaud's description of methods of escape open to Napoleon, adding, "He has repeated this nonsense on every streetcorner in Jamestown—together with his assurances that he would never betray his Emperor!" Apparently Balmain, among others even higher placed than he, had been persuaded to put Gourgaud down as an ass, which was perhaps excusable enough under the circumstances. But the generals made by Napoleon had been selected for their promotion because of outstanding ability in the field, for intelligence and courage, and even beyond those virtues for the faculty of being "lucky"—fortunate in their undertakings.

It might be concluded then, that if Baron Gourgaud played the fool in public, it was perhaps because he wanted to be taken for a fool. The machinery of state, close scrutiny and heavy-handed supervision might well be relaxed somewhat for an obvious ass, one who would inevitably leave a plainly marked trail behind him in carrying out no matter what fantastically conceived enterprises. Sir Hudson Lowe, however, recorded no such reservations; he sent a letter to Lord Bathurst calculated to ensure the French officer a most favorable reception. From the evidence Lowe seems to have been won over more completely than any other and had been exceedingly friendly and obliging to a man whom he was compelled to regard officially as a renegade—albeit one well justified.

At all events the French had succeeded in getting their emissary into England—fairly rapidly, smoothly, and in an atmosphere favorable to the execution of their plan—whatever it was.

He was not going to be permitted to land in France, however, although there is little reason to believe that he had ever seriously anticipated that such a relaxation of the laws against proscripted men would be made in his case. It mattered very little apparently—England was close enough for his purposes, easily accessible to Bonapartist sympathizers from across the Channel. From the first, old partisans sought out his lodgings in London, ostensibly to receive the firsthand news of their hero but secretly eager to learn the real reason for the journey and the elaborate hocus-pocus of publicity being woven about the apparent defalcation of one of the Emperor's trusted aides. These private meetings were going on even as Gourgaud continued to supply Lord Bathurst with more of the same sort of slanted half-truths and specious falsehoods he had indulged in at Plantation House.

But beyond the point where these fantastic revelations might assist his cause, he steadfastly refused to be drawn: Bathurst's secretary Goulburn wrote to his superior on May 20, 1818, that "Gourgaud refuses to charge either Balcombe or Dr. O'Meara [with acting as intermediaries in Napoleon's illicit correspondence]." "The numerous communications are facilitated by inhabitants and soldiers." Both Lowe and Bathurst were convinced that the two men named were heavily involved, and were trying very hard to obtain testimony to support their belief. It is seen that even to strengthen his own case the general would not be drawn into betraying the men who had been friends to Longwood from the beginning; as for the "betrayal" of his master, that was the key Napoleon had authorized him to employ, whereby he would be able to open the prison doors, and little the great strategist cared as

EXITS AND AN ENTRANCE

to what the world made of these sixpenny "revelations"—all that would take care of itself later.

Accordingly, in the course of the first few weeks after his arrival in London, the task that Gourgaud had been sent to carry out, or to supervise, was successfully effected. It had been discovered and was officially noted that known Jacobins and French secret agents frequented his quarters. From these quarters and with these agents he was able to accomplish, in those few weeks, the task that had exasperated the French on St. Helena—not because of its difficulty, necessarily, but because of the inordinate lapse of time between exchanges of letters, because of letters that failed to arrive, because of the danger of putting on paper, which might be intercepted, actual objectives and names.

At last he received the intelligence that the thing was done and nothing was left for him to do—from then on all would be in the hands of Fate and the Emperor himself. The hateful masquerade in which he had been engaged had served its full purpose and could be abandoned. To a man of honor, a distinguished soldier and a confidant of the Emperor, the part he played must have become a loathsome one: In the very heart of the land of his traditional enemies—those men cold-eyed and noncommittal, the persecutors of his idol—he had played his assigned role, all too conscious of the revulsion his conduct created even in the hearts of those most anxious to take advantage of his every sordid communication. The time had arrived when he might safely abandon the deception—and in the typical Gourgaud fashion he acted, impetuously and with enthusiasm. In a series of letters to be made public he denied all of his former allegations and "revelations"—the entire nauseous structure!

It is possible to sense, even after all the years, the relief that burned in the heart and countenance of this excellent officer as he found himself once more able to "stare down" the chilly glances of

WHO LIES HERE?

the supercilious, to reassume his rightful stature as a distinguished and honorable soldier working in the midst of his peers. All very well, of course, but the British ministry was hardly to be blamed for failing to appreciate this latest *volte-face*, and the manner in which they had been taken in—for what obscure purposes they were unable to guess. Their earlier belief—that this general was not only a fool but somewhat unbalanced into the bargain—was reinforced. They promptly expelled him from England, of course, and he departed for Hamburg, there to reside with the aid of a pension thoughtfully provided for him by Napoleon through his son-in-law Prince Eugène.

The day on which Gourgaud had found himself able to announce his emancipation was August 25, 1818.

On this day he sent a letter to the ex-Empress Marie Louise, telling her something of the truth concerning actual conditions at Longwood, of the miserable treatment accorded her husband. This was soon to be published in English and European papers, as were yet others addressed to the Czar Alexander and to the Austrian Emperor. In these letters he got in some heavy salvos against Sir Hudson Lowe—which shows that he had well comprehended that official's assumed affability, and that he continued to despise the man as all at Longwood had learned to do.

This startingly abrupt and complete resumption of his soldierly integrity by an apparent renegade, in the presence of his enemies, is the best proof one might desire that the obscure errand on which he had been sent after that elaborate preparation had been successfully carried out. The date, too, has its own peculiar significance and should be held well in mind as the changing phenomena of St. Helena are further observed.

As for the nature of Gourgaud's mission itself, at this point we can only conclude that it was one impossible to conduct satisfactorily at such long range and with such comparatively insecure

EXITS AND AN ENTRANCE

communications; it was one either sufficiently complex or so charged with unforeseeable contingencies and alternatives as to require the nearby presence of a resourceful and energetic agent —one charged with full authority to make all decisions on whatever points might arise. And in the meanwhile the evident fact is that while in the Americas men were conspiring with admirable devotion and ingenuity at the ramifications of their obscure plots for freeing the Emperor and bringing him in triumph to the New World—that master strategist, confiding himself to the plans of no lesser men, had already made his play and was now preparing for the final consummation.

General Gourgaud was fully aware that his arrangements had been completed, a task carried out—or he could not have dared to reveal himself so rashly and completely. Having done so, he was free to go about his own affairs once more—either in seeking out his own enjoyment or in making the necessary contacts for the furtherance of his career, as he saw fit. It is on record that after 1821, when the French were permitted to leave St. Helena and to return to France—Gourgaud, Montholon and Bertrand were often gathered together in Paris, and in the greatest of apparent amity and good-fellowship. All the insults and calumnies they had once so bitterly devised for one another now seemed wholly forgotten in the pleasures of renewing their great memories—and in the mutual enjoyment of their colossal secret.

During this period those who knew them openly asserted what is implied in the preceding paragraphs—that Gourgaud's secret mission, wherewith he had been charged by the Emperor himself, obliged him to represent himself as the enemy of Napoleon in order that he might gain the confidence of the British and French ministries and so be permitted to travel in France or at the least to live in London: in brief, to do as it is known that he did. He had at first enthusiastically surpassed his instructions, as indicated by

WHO LIES HERE?

Montholon's cautionary note of 1818. His diary likewise, in its first edition at least, teemed with "awkward phrases"—these designed for Lowe's benefit should it have been confiscated, thus further convincing the governor by this material written long before that his contempt and dislike of the Longwood people, as well as of Napoleon himself, were of long standing. In later editions of this work, as French biographers attest, most of these expressions are deleted.

Arresting also, in addition to the renewed comradeship among the three, is the way in which Montholon and Bertrand went about ensuring that Gourgaud receive compensation for the fact that he was not—as obviously he could not have been—mentioned in the Emperor's will. This had been an unavoidable stumbling block, since Napoleon could hardly appear to have so soon forgiven his officer for the great damage the latter had tried to do him. Both Montholon and Bertrand, however, testified in Paris to having received an oral command from their master—a "verbal and secret legacy" had been provided for Gourgaud. Their generosity and good will is particularly in evidence here, since by providing a share for Gourgaud their own specified legacies would be proportionately reduced—and even more so when it was later discovered that there was insufficient money in Napoleon's estate to meet fully the provisions of the will.

At any rate it may surely be presumed that the strongest bonds of friendship prevailed between these comrades of St. Helena, and a proper enjoyment of a shared mystery was divined by their intimates and so recorded in their correspondence. Formal historians must offer another explanation for this rapprochement, holding to the opinion that these three had agreed among themselves that all old antipathies should be forgotten and smoothed over, so that their prestige in the eyes of the world might be

EXITS AND AN ENTRANCE

maintained and critics deprived of an opportunity to cast mud on the great legend, or to disparage its principals.

The tale of William Balcombe, purveyor of supplies to Longwood's people and the next after Gourgaud to leave the island, affords one of the less unpleasant commentaries on the exile. He, his wife and their four children became the Emperor's earliest and best friends on St. Helena, for during the months when Longwood was being prepared for the occupancy of the French Napoleon had shared their home and enjoyed their highly informal hospitality.

In her *Saint Helena Story* Dame Mabel Brookes has told most charmingly of this earliest period, a good deal of the flavor of her narrative deriving from the diary of her ancestress and Napoleon's loyal comrade—Betsy, the younger of the two Balcombe girls—as well as from anecdotes handed down in her family. She has told me that William Balcombe was positive of the presence of Napoleon at Longwood up to the time of his own departure on March 18, 1818; indeed, he had received the impression that the Emperor was disinclined to consider the question of escape, since he could imagine no place of residence where he would be free of the fear of assassination by Bourbon or other enemy agents. He had added that he would only return to France if and when the French people invited him to do so—otherwise he would prefer above everything else to be allowed to live privately in England.

Still placating England! Of course it was politic to do so, or to appear to do so—even though his secret plan for escape was already on the way to its implementation. By every possible means the British were to be lulled and pacified, their suspicions dulled and their indifference encouraged: That, too, was part of the plan; even to Balcombe, whom he liked and trusted, he spoke at cross-purposes, feeling that some of his remarks at least might find their way to Lowe's ears and do their minute quota of good. The departure of the Balcombes, owing to Lowe's increasing animus against them, was a blow to Napoleon, in practical as well as emotional ways. They were gentlefolk. (William was rumored to be a natural son of George III, and unquestionably he had a certain obscure influence at court; in addition, William had been a naval officer.) And because of the many necessary visits to Longwood in regard to the provisioning, Balcombe, without any doubt, was entrusted with carrying out secret commissions, bearing illicit communications both to and from "General Bonaparte."

Fifteen-year-old Betsy had been an always cheerful and enlivening visitor at Longwood—one who may have gradually developed a schoolgirl "crush" on the world-famed figure who appeared so genuinely to enjoy her ingenuous and often hopelessly disrespectful conversations. In this unlikely friendship a long-submerged aspect of Napoleon's character—one altogether human and appealing—made its abrupt appearance: He clowned, played blindman's buff and sought out the children daily when he was living at The Briars to share in their activities and games; the pastry chef made up exotic confections for their delight, while Betsy and her older sister, Jane, tried to teach Napoleon English. Here was a man, quite obviously, who had never had the time for childhood and its freedom from care.

Of course, after the coming of the splenetic Hudson Lowe, all this lighthearted enjoyment had to cease. Balcombe early fell into disfavor for his apparent partisanship and evidences of friendship for the exiles; soon he, and Betsy as well because of her continued visiting at Longwood, came under suspicion of aiding in the transmission of letters to and from the French. The aging French commissioner, the Marquis de Montchenu—an egregious ass who nevertheless could see how the wind blew and wanted

EXITS AND AN ENTRANCE

to curry favor with Lowe for the sake of his good dinners—sent back a scandalous report on Napoleon's relationship with his young English friend. This item was published in the French newspapers and was ultimately drawn to William's attention. He at once challenged Montchenu to a duel—which so terrified the old roué that he promised to have a retraction published under his name, and did so. But this and other hectic scenes, particularly with Lowe, had convinced Balcombe that it would be the better part of wisdom to apply for a long leave of absence in England, lest the time should come when the choice should no longer be his to make and the entire family be put under arrest and sent back in disgrace. His judgment was quite correct, as events were to demonstrate, for Lowe's mental instability was rapidly coming to the fore under the stress of his anxieties. The Balcombe family sailed only ten days after General Gourgaud's departure, and because of Lowe's animosity they were never to return.

With increasing momentum the company of the faithful was dispersing, and now the Emperor had lost not only a valued companionship in this place so devoid of opportunities for such amenities, but in addition what may have been one of the principal modes of contact between the French and the world at large. Some indication of the truth of this took place on September 19 of that year, when a case of books addressed to Dr. O'Meara, then in disgrace also, fell into the governor's hands. Together Lowe and Thomas Reade, the head of Lowe's intelligence and his chief spy, proceeded to pry open the case, shaking out each volume for possible enclosures.

True enough, concealed in some of the books were letters whose phrases, referring obscurely to many suspicious-sounding operations, nevertheless plainly involved William Balcombe by name. (At the time of shipping the books London had not heard of O'Meara's dismissal and his sailing from St. Helena.) There was a

WHO LIES HERE?

letter from Balcombe implying that he was actively working in London "for his friends on the island," while large sums of money were mentioned in connection with announced transactions involving General Bertrand—amounting in all to 395,000 francs. Something was in the wind indeed, even in London itself! It is known that Bertrand had, with prudent foresight, transferred a large fortune to a London bank before he had embarked from France with the Emperor; moreover, there was a reference in one of the letters to a recent visit made to the banking house of Lafitte, in Paris—this connected in some manner with the large sums of money before alluded to.

All very tantalizing, but not too informative for Lowe—except as concerned Balcombe's certain involvement. Lowe at once forwarded the letters to Bathurst together with a strong denunciation of the ex-provisioner of Longwood, and after this exposure it seems quite miraculous that the friendly William was to be given—after an extensive period of idleness—another well-paid position, this time in far-away Australia. Perhaps he *did* possess that secret influence at court that gossip had attributed to him! He had been a kindly friend to a man stripped of power and lost among strangers: His memory deserves a salute.

The account of the Balcombes belongs here not only because the departures of 1818 are being reviewed, but because it affords some insight into Napoleon's private postal service and its ramifications, as well as demonstrating the comparative ease with which Lowe's restrictions were bypassed. However, it illustrates as well a dangerous weakness in the system such as obliged Gourgaud to return to Europe as an instructed plenipotentiary, acting on the spot: the ever-present danger of crucially important messages falling into the wrong hands—all unbeknown to the intended recipient, as well as to the writer himself.

* * *

EXITS AND AN ENTRANCE

There were no more departures until June 18, and these were from the Longwood "service"—the chef, LePage, with his wife and daughter, and Bertrand's servant, Heymann, with his wife and son. Since the two women were also employees, it would appear that the serving staff was becoming somewhat attenuated. None of these people were to be allowed to land in England, but after a brief term of residence in Hamburg they were permitted to return to France in February of 1819. France has ever given a favorable reception to a good cook—and LePage had been chef for King Joseph, Napoleon's brother, before taking service with the Emperor.

On July 3 the Austrian commissioner, Baron von Stürmer, left St. Helena, having been recalled by a government grown impatient of the reports of continual badgering and questionings to which their representative had been subjected by the governor; Lowe suspected everyone, of course, and not least the foreign commissioners, whom he grilled at frequent intervals—trying to catch them out in a deception. Beyond this treatment there was the fact that in all the time Stürmer had been on the island, neither he nor the other two commissioners had ever once succeeded in so much as setting eyes on the man whose presence he had so expensively been sent to verify. That statement is in itself an adequate endorsement for the system of palace protocol in force at Longwood, and of its complete impregnability. The Austrian government now invited the Frenchman, the Marquis de Montchenu, to represent it in addition to his own country on St. Helena—something he was only too glad to undertake since he complained continually of his inadequate pay and the extremely high cost of living on the island. After this economical fusion of roles had been effected, the Baron von Stürmer was sent to be Austrian consul in the United States—a much livelier post, and

WHO LIES HERE?

one located about as far from Sir Hudson as could conveniently be established.

Dr. Barry O'Meara had long been under the active menace of the axe's edge. His presence, as physician to Napoleon, has already been accounted for, and mention made of his somewhat dubious position between the Emperor and Lowe in regard to carrying privileged communications to either of these men—in violation of professional ethics, without doubt, but at the same time with no intent beyond that of playing the good fellow and keeping everyone happy. It is uncertain yet just how much harm he may have done by his indiscretions or deliberate attempts to curry favor.

The conversations he reported to Lowe were innocuous enough in general; they had the effect, however, of sharpening the governor's appetite for even richer fare, and he bethought himself of the wonderful advantages of having a really loquacious doctor installed at Longwood—one willing to act the spy completely and to keep him posted daily as to the thoughts and comments deriving from the very source of all his concern. The failure of this idea to appeal to O'Meara and the knowledge of a series of small favors done by the physician for the French was then quite sufficient to produce an eruption of violent denunciation and an atmosphere of hateful domination directed against the Irishman. Not only was the doctor dismissed from the island, but from the very service itself—his name was struck from the Navy list at Lowe's representations.

It was established that he had publicly charged Lowe with desiring the death of his prisoner, with having made plain to the doctor himself how such an event would be to Britain's benefit; O'Meara made it clear that Lowe had actually urged him to effect Napoleon's demise by the administration of poison or by with-

EXITS AND AN ENTRANCE

holding proper treatment in an emergency. This, of course, was a most damning charge, and since it could not possibly be proven, and was obviously extremely unlikely, the doctor's disgrace and downfall were inevitable.

O'Meara was, however, a fighter, and he refused to take this treatment lying down. His ultimate revenge was to be spectacular, for his famous book *A Voice from St. Helena,* besides making him a fortune, stirred up a current of public revulsion against Hudson Lowe that was eventually to bear him down to ruin.

On August 2, 1818, the *Griffin* bore Dr. O'Meara away from Jamestown and directly to England and a court of enquiry; the place he left vacant was not to be filled for nine months, and then only intermittently by casually selected Army surgeons making infrequent calls at Longwood. Each of these was to experience the humiliation and exasperation of Lowe's interference or interrogation, until at the last the utterly incompetent Antommarchi was sent out by Napoleon's mother to be Longwood's resident "physician."

That there was, or had been, collusion of a kind favorable to Napoleon between Balcombe and O'Meara seems sufficiently established—confirmed especially by that last letter that Lowe intercepted, hidden amidst the books.

On August 22 Count Alexander Antinovich Ramsay de Balmain, the commissioner of Czar Alexander, left rather impulsively for a holiday in Rio de Janeiro. This urbane and aristocratic career diplomat was considerably the superior of either of his colleagues, the Austrian and French representatives, in stature and ability. His regular reports sent home for the benefit of his government and Alexander—and which that monarch perused with great enjoyment, as his minister informed Balmain—were full of interest and the shrewdest of comment on the local situation. His admiration for Napoleon's performance was always in evidence in these letters, quite freely expressed and in a manner that shows he knew such a sentiment would be agreeable to his master; he referred often to the way in which the prisoner preserved his dignity and air of historical integrity under the unworthy regime established by his captors. The latter part of the Russian's name, the "Ramsay de Balmain," tells of a Scottish ancestry; no doubt but that the dry humor evident in many of his reports, especially in those having to do with the stupidity or inconsequence of some of Lowe's measures, or to his colleagues' erratic behavior, was one of the characteristics of his heritage. According to the historical record he—no more than his two companions in frustration—was never to set eyes on the famous Longwood tenant, except perhaps through a telescope from afar.

In this consideration of the departures of 1818 the crucial period—the last days of August— has been passed. Now comes a seemingly minor episode in which may be perceived the first indication of a radical change having taken place in the character and nature of the master of Longwood.

On December 18, 1818, Pierron and Ali, members of the "service," went to Plantation House seeking the governor's permission to leave St. Helena. Pierron had been appointed to take the place of LePage as chef since the latter's departure in June; "Ali" was the name given to one Louis Etienne Saint-Denis, so rebaptized when he was chosen to succeed to the position of "Mameluke" to the Emperor—this a post originating in the Egyptian days, when Napoleon had brought home a squadron of them to ornament his Guard with their Oriental costume and dashing horsemanship. The personal Mameluke was a sort of valet, however, and even so was Ali—including in his duties some transcription of his master's dictation, occasional service as a

EXITS AND AN ENTRANCE

groom, and ultimately those of dining-room servant and librarian. In later years he was to offer some recollections of St. Helena in his book of memoirs. These are of small value save in some of the areas of his competence.

When LePage and Heymann with their families had sought permission in June to quit the island, they had made the error of doing so without first informing Napoleon of their intention. As soon as he was made aware of this *lèse majesté,* he discharged them instantly and did not see them again before their departure, being utterly incensed at this breach of decorum. But December of the same year, the incident repeated itself—permission to approach Lowe was not sought by Ali and Pierron; yet when the news of their visit to the governor's mansion reached their master's ears, he made no objection and did—nothing. Not even as a gesture to impress the British! A profound change in the man to have been effected in only six months.

At the end of this year Madame Bertrand was especially despondent and continually reproached her patient husband with the deplorable nature of their circumstances—wholly cut off from the good society in which they had reveled while at Paris—the costs of their lavish entertainment were reputed to have amounted to more than two million francs a year—the children growing up cultureless and without any proper education, the general's career the more blemished the longer they remained remote from the centers of civilization: An endless list, for Fanny felt her beauty passing, and like all the others she was supremely bored. Madame Montholon was also speaking, quite openly now, of returning to Europe, and both ladies made repeated assaults on their husbands' selfish resolution to continue on in their intolerable exile. La Montholon also complained of her failing health and told of her urgent need to seek out appropriate medical springs and

WHO LIES HERE?

specialized European medical care. At last Montholon weakened and let fall some hints that he might agree to accompany her; later yet even the faithful Grand Marshal was to crumble in his resolution and to speak of the possibility of his own departure.

The fact that both of these gentlemen were under technical sentences of death in France no doubt served greatly to temper their discontent with the despised island and the monotony of their service. But beyond even this consideration was the matter of Napoleon's fortune, reputed to be a considerable one, and from which he had promised rich rewards to those who should stay with him to the end. If they were mercenary in this, who shall blame them? Theirs was a situation few men would envy, or enter upon without strong assurances of reward; as for loyalty their conduct from Waterloo on was sufficient evidence of it—after all, they could have gone to America as so many other French officers after the collapse of the Empire.

Nevertheless, after protracted and persistent efforts to obtain her permission to leave, Madame Montholon sailed from Jamestown harbor on July 22 of the next year—1819: She would have been gone long before had not Lowe, for his own obscure reasons, been obdurate. She had at the last experienced some little difficulty, in contrast to the situation earlier, in persuading the Count to stay on and thus secure their financial future. For several months prior to his wife's leaving, Montholon had been engaged in a vigorous campaign of "buttering up" the French commissioner—no doubt with the object of having this official send a glowing report on him to his government, thus to facilitate his return to his native land. No such happy result eventuated, however, and this failure, in combination with his good lady's objections to his leaving, served to reconcile the Count to his lot.

* * *

EXITS AND AN ENTRANCE

One more departure from Longwood must be included with all these others, although it was through the portals of death and not merely the rocky headlands of Jamestown harbor that the traveler passed.

Cipriani Franceschi was officially classified as *maître d'hôtel* of the Emperor's household. He had attained to this position by means not well understood. He was a Corsican, and it appears likely that there had been a traditional relationship between his family and that of the Bonapartes—his son and daughter were in the service of Cardinal Fesch and Madame Letitia respectively—Napoleon's mother and uncle. Cipriani, as he was known to everyone, was shrewd and conniving as well as thoroughgoing in his hatreds and allegiances, with a long memory for his wrongs. He had served as a spy when the French retook Capri from the British in 1808—and the officer entrusted with its defense had been none other than Hudson Lowe. The uninspired efforts of the latter had occasioned unflattering comment from his superiors, and it is believed that Lowe knew of Cipriani's considerable role in his humiliation, and of his identity. Whether he was also aware that the Cipriani of Longwood was the same one who had aided in the debacle of Capri is less certain, although it is unlikely that such a man as Sir Thomas Reade—Lowe's assiduous chief of police and longtime military associate—would have overlooked the connection.

Cipriani had been one of the volunteers to accompany Napoleon to Elba, but soon afterward he was to be found in dubious residence in Vienna, whence he forwarded to his master the up-to-date reports of those deliberations of the Congress that would be of concern to him. One of these items told of the proposal of Napoleon's old minister, Talleyrand, that St. Helena would, even then, be a more appropriate place of detention for the fallen Emperor than was Elba. This report of Cipriani's had been one of the chief factors influencing Napoleon's decision to return to France—there had seemed little else he might do and yet preserve his comparative degree of freedom.

Cipriani appears to have been held in a very high regard by his master, who closeted himself, at Longwood, frequently and for lengthy periods with his diligent and astute servitor—often to the resentment of the jealous officers of the household. By means best known to himself alone, the majordomo had established in Jamestown his own network of informers and counteragents, a task for which he was well fitted by his endowment of an ingratiating manner and air of genial bonhomie. His activities were without doubt of the greatest use to his master—but they were attracting the unfavorable attention of the British, who felt themselves to be incommoded by them; Lowe very soon recognized that this man's insatiable energy—displayed in the outwitting of his guards, in the gathering and dissemination of rumors, in the continual vague furthering of ends no doubt insidious and most certainly irritating—was an increasing threat to his peace of mind, to say the least.

On February 23, 1818, while serving at the dining table, the Corsican was suddenly stricken by the most excruciating pains in the abdomen, falling to the floor in agonized convulsions; the primitive treatment of the time could afford no alleviation, and the wretched man expired on the afternoon of February 27. The diagnosis agreed on by O'Meara and two British army physicians called in for consultation was "inflammation of the bowels"; no autopsy was performed, and Cipriani was interred in St. Paul's churchyard, close by Plantation House. He was borne to his grave by the French officers and some few British, but not by Napoleon: This was out of bounds for him unless he consented to being escorted by a guard—a humiliation he had long before refused to accept.

EXITS AND AN ENTRANCE

Napoleon was overwhelmed by his servant's shocking fate and rendered more than usually gloomy by its implications: The fear of assassination was never very far from his awareness. Often he described attempts made in the past to poison him. Now he examined the kitchen minutely, inquiring closely into its customs and practices, openly giving vent to his suspicions of the startlingly sudden collapse of his majordomo. It is not unlikely that O'Meara may have mentioned to him his story regarding Lowe's sinister hints as to the advantages to the world of Napoleon's demise.

Cipriani had been one of the prime movers in the escape from Elba; it could be that once again, by the sacrifice of death, this loyal servant to the Emperor confirmed him in his committal to the second attempt: Shortly after the interment Gourgaud was started off on the road leading him to England.

Napoleon spent a considerable sum of money—one source describes it as "a fortune," while another gives the figure of fourteen hundred gold francs—for the burial and the erection of an ornate marble monument over the grave of Cipriani. No one can tell what happened to this monument, or when—it has vanished and the grave as well, although Monsieur Martineau, the French consul on St. Helena, points out that many other stones of the same period and earlier are still in position in the churchyard today. It is well known that the presence of poison in the stomach or bowel contents may be determined for an indefinite period after death; under the circumstances one cannot help wondering why there was no autopsy ordered. Not too long, one suspects, after Cipriani's burial, someone had made very certain that such an investigation would never be made. The facts of this case are incontrovertible and not readily explicable: To this day the truth of Cipriani's death is veiled in mystery and obscured by a terrible suspicion.

Such were the departures from St. Helena during the year

WHO LIES HERE?

1818—with the exception of the most significant of all. According to all indications it probably took place near the end of the month of August. It is now in order to examine the strange incidents and references that combine to suggest that hereabouts a turning point in Longwood's history must have taken place. Each of the facts in this series is thought-provoking in itself, but cumulatively they demand attention and the historian's reappraisal of his material, in the name of a responsible devotion to the truth.

By the middle of 1819 the French at Longwood had been reduced in numbers by almost half—almost all having left in the previous year. Many of those yet remaining were showing signs of wishing to follow the example that had been set them, but were deterred either by fear of the nature of their reception in Europe or of losing the anticipated rewards of their full term of service. Of them all, the decent Bertrand, the opportunist but kindly Montholon, and the faithful valet Marchand continued to the end to comport themselves with the most praiseworthy appearance of consideration and the kindliest simulation of deference and duty.

One of the chief difficulties to be overcome in the impartial consideration of these new insights is that many of them have from the beginning been assigned other values entirely, and in an almost opposite context—that of the accepted dogma of St. Helena. Thus regarded, they are inevitably liable to dismissal, by the more stolid-witted, into the limbo of "known facts" and historical truths. Such people refuse to permit themselves to perceive that any one of these incidents might be a unit in a mosaic quite other than the more obvious one, promptly scrapping it with the impatient comment, "Oh, that's easily accounted for in the

EXITS AND AN ENTRANCE

standard framework, because—!" Then follows the stock account that formal historians have provided from the only records available to them or interpretable by them. In this instance the records are those "inside" stories of the French companions—Montholon, Bertrand, Marchand. These, it cannot be too often repeated, are the principal significant accounts of the period 1818 to the end in 1821—the accounts from within the walls of Longwood, where the British never penetrated to make those "hour-by-hour, night-and-day" observations of their prisoner. There is literally no other material written by eyewitnesses and from within Longwood's walls, for this period—because there could not be. Las Cases and Gourgaud, as pointed out, can write only of the period before then—when Napoleon was yet present, in *propria persona*—as does Dr. O'Meara. If Bertrand, Montholon and Marchand were obliged to make their histories agree, in carrying out their joint purpose—would this not have been the simplest of tasks, especially concerning an environment in which so very little actually occurred, day by day?

So our current beliefs have been contrived and molded because there exist no other sources of new information for this period. But there do exist a series of clues—some of those "loose ends" earlier referred to, which inevitably attract the eye and the curiosity of those chronically dissatisfied with the apparently seamless structure of much accepted history. It was Napoleon who defined history as "a lie agreed on."

A good example with which to commence, demonstrating at the same time the principle whereby an inconvenient or difficult story is forced into the acceptable mold because there is no other way of including it as it stands, is one concerning Madame Mère and her strange "delusions" of 1818 and thereafter.

In October of 1818 Letitia told her daughter-in-law Catherine, the wife of ex-King Jerome, "Napoleon is on his way to Malta!"

WHO LIES HERE?

Both she and her half-brother Cardinal Fesch became at this time firmly persuaded of the fact that the Emperor was no longer on St. Helena. They demonstrated the sincerity of their belief by responding to a request for servants for Longwood—specifically a cook, a doctor and a priest—with a delay of over a year before at last dispatching on a leisurely route a shameful collection of incompetents. They consisted of a so-called "Doctor" Antommarchi—in reality an assistant to an anatomist, a dissector merely; there was a servant of whom it was said at Longwood that "he didn't even know how to brew coffee"—he was sent as an assistant cook; of two priests one was old and gout-ridden, both simpleminded and tongue-tied, the other but a country boor. The comment of their employer was, when at long last they arrived: "It would have been impossible to have made a worse selection!"

Madame Mère, the one-time Letitia Bonaparte, had acquired much of the art of gracious living, thanks to her son's genius; she had never, however, been able to overcome her frugal Corsican habit of mind, her realization of the evanescence of riches. Now, since this much-loved son was no longer a prisoner in the South Atlantic, why should she spend good money on sending out first-class people such as she would otherwise have insisted upon for him, had he still been a helpless exile there? Why should she even bother to hurry these people on their way? Hence, logically enough, the unlikely and eminently unsuitable choice of personnel, which was not to arrive in Jamestown until September of 1819.

But how do the conventional histories account for her extraordinary belief, her uncharacteristic action? There is, of course, only one way in which to do so, and that is to declare that she had become simpleminded! And Cardinal Fesch? He was similarly afflicted, of course. It must have been so, even if the Cardinal was only in his mid-fifties and Letitia, that epitome of practicality and

EXITS AND AN ENTRANCE

common sense, had yet almost twenty years of activity and interest before her. They had fallen, it is further explained, under the influence of a clairvoyant and fortune-teller who systematically deluded them for her own ends, and from whose influence they were later to free themselves. This addition was rendered desirable because there is no other evidence of the mental collapse of either of these strong-minded individuals.

It is easier to believe that this fortune-teller was the intermediary between Napoleon and his mother: Such would have been an excellent choice for the purpose.

Here are two letters that Napoleon's mother wrote just prior to this period. They are hardly the productions of a mind gone soft or become receptive to delusions. The first was addressed to the assembled potentates of Europe, at the Congress of Aix-la-Chapelle:

> A mother, more bowed with grief than words can tell, has long been hoping that your Imperial and Royal Highnesses would give her back her life. It is impossible that the captivity of the Emperor Napoleon should not come up for discussion. Your magnanimity, your power, and your memory of earlier events, will surely incline your Imperial and Royal Majesties to work for the liberation of a prince for whom you once professed friendship. I pray to God, and you, for you are God's representatives on earth. Interests of State have their limits. Posterity, which confers immortality, admires a generous conqueror.

A little later she was accused of having provided millions of francs for a scheme designed to liberate her son, and the Pope

WHO LIES HERE?

himself despatched his secretary to demand of her the truth. She replied to this gentleman as follows:

> Tell the Pope—and may the monarchs mark my words: If I were so fortunate as to possess all these millions they have credited me with, I should certainly not spend them in buying champions for my son's cause. He has enough of them already! I would, rather, equip a fleet capable of rescuing him from the island where he is unjustly detained.

A good, tough, resolute answer, becoming to the temper of an Emperor's mother.

This concept she had entertained, that her son was in October of 1818 nearing Malta on his way to northern Italy, is at least as easy to consider as the other view of her statement—that the shrewd Fesch and the practical and wise Letitia had suddenly become half-witted. The date, moreover, harmonizes well with that latter end of August which preoccupies us—considering the usual time of a passage from St. Helena through the Mediterranean. But the reluctance to shrug off an old viewpoint and to accept a new is well illustrated here. There could easily be more plausible explanations for a good many such incidents, which, conventionally, must be accounted for in a highly artificial and strained manner—simply because there appeared to be no other way in which they could conveniently be handled.

It is notable that late in the year of 1818 tales such as this had become rather common, both on the Continent and in England. Why, just at that particular time, were they so numerous and so persistent that some newspapers apparently felt themselves called on to comment on them editorially?

EXITS AND AN ENTRANCE

In addition to the proliferation of the stories of contemplated rescue previously commented on, there was a certain amount of indiscreet gossip originating in Longwood itself—such as a well-publicized remark the Emperor had let fall on the occasion of his forty-eighth birthday party, given him on August 15, 1817. He hoped, he had said, that when his next birthday anniversary arrived he would no longer be on the island. Although this was let fall, without doubt, with a perfect innocence of any extended or implied meaning, certain long ears among the Longwood "service" caught it up and gave it currency as far as Plantation House—where the glowering Lowe seized on it in his usual heavy-handed manner. Yet if the remark had been the unguarded expression of a maturing plan—or even a deliberate one—adequate advance notice was being given to all concerned, with a touch of humor perhaps.

There were, later on, some references to a letter now difficult to trace, written by Madame Bertrand to a relative residing in Russia. It began: "My dear Caroline, at last we have triumphed—Success is ours; Napoleon has left the island!" The date was that on which Gourgaud had performed his astounding about-face in London, negating all his previous testimony against Napoleon: It was written on August 25 and obviously smuggled off the island in the usual fashion.

The degree of concern prevailing in the British ministry is evident in a letter from Lord Bathurst to Lowe at the end of 1818, containing this paragraph: "I was particularly struck with that part of the conversation in which Count Montholon states that General Bonaparte is never seen, and that he defies the governor to say for certain that General Bonaparte is still at Longwood, *or has been there for the last two months.*" The italics are my own. All such statements as this one of Montholon's soon became public knowledge and were rapidly disseminated across the Continent. In the

WHO LIES HERE?

same key exactly was a report sent to the potentates assembled at Aix-la-Chapelle, containing the phrase that states:

> . . . a plan of escape has been discussed by the persons of his suite—and could have been carried out had not Napoleon preferred to defer its execution. Bonaparte's familiars boast that the question of his presence on the island is a mystery to all, even to the governor.

Surely these two statements, which are a part of the Lowe Papers in the British Museum, should be sufficient to inspire at the very least a slight uncertainty in the mind of even the most devoted believer in historical infallibility? But there are more yet.

From this time on there was a determined effort made by the British, under Lowe's prodding, to get a proper look at the man they were supposed to be guarding—an effort that never ceased, yet was never rewarded. The orderly officer attached to Longwood as the official liaison between the French and their captors became the object of a permanent conspiracy, the aim of which was to frustrate this devoted man in his daily attempts to carry out his duty. At this period the officer was a Captain Nicholls, whose instructions were, primarily, to report to Plantation House that he had either seen Napoleon that day or had done his best to obtain a view of him. In all weathers he went prowling about Longwood's grounds, the principal occupant seeming to take a malicious pleasure in effectively concealing himself or in misleading the unhappy officer with false messages relayed through one of the servants.

On a certain day in July of 1819, for example, after a series of failures that had gone on for so long that he was becoming self-conscious about his ineffectiveness, Captain Nicholls reported to Major Gorrequer, Lowe's aide on duty at the time: "At this

EXITS AND AN ENTRANCE

moment there is a person sitting in the General's dining room with a cocked hat on. I, however, can only see the hat moving about. If the French are accustomed to sit at dinner with a hat on, probably this is Napoleon Bonaparte at dinner." No doubt Major Gorrequer recognized the note of desperation in this report, for he sent back the accommodating answer: "There is in fact no other person of the establishment at Longwood in the habit of wearing a cocked hat, and consequently it is more than likely that you did see him." On the contrary, it is more than likely that he had *not* seen the Emperor, by that late date; that famous silhouette was to be accepted on occasion after occasion as the veritable Corsican himself. But Nicholls' report is very illuminating, both as to the desperate lack of intelligence the British possessed with regard to the situation at Longwood and to the vague doubts that were creeping in among them about the actual identity of their prisoner.

That officialdom shared in a suspicion of something being indeterminately wrong about the imprisonment they were supervising is implicit in the cautious wording of many reports, such as this one of Captain Nicholls (almost offensive in its desperate indifference) and many of his other accountings. For another example there was a Dr. Arnott's first report—he an army surgeon accepted in desperation by the Longwood people because none other was available except the grossly incompetent Antommarchi who had requested that a consultant be sent for. Arnott's first visit to Longwood was made at nine in the evening, and he discovered his patient lying in a chamber unlit except for the dim radiance afforded by shaded candles in an adjacent room. His description of this professional visit begins: "The room was so dark that I could not see him, but I felt him, or *someone else*. I took his pulse, etc." The italics are the doctor's.

On July 20, 1819, there is a report made by Lowe: "Napoleon

WHO LIES HERE?

has not left the house for one hundred days." There had been two months of such invisibility reported after August of the preceding year. Was this period of vanishment to provide the new tenant with an opportunity for undisturbed rehearsal, the gaining of confidence in his role? The "person with a cocked hat on" might well have become rusty in the life-and-death part he was to perform before the most critical of audiences, with lives and eternal fame all dependent on the skill of his impersonation! After O'Meara's dismissal in August of '18 the prisoner was only rarely seen outside, and when the orderly officer complained to Montholon about his inability to obtain any sightings, the count informed him that "the Emperor was unwell and did not rise from his bed save for a couple of hours each day."

However, with Montholon's assistance various ruses were employed whereby a glimpse of the invalid might occasionally be obtained—the Bertrand children were encouraged to play in front of his bedroom window, and their cries nearly always brought him briefly into view; or the count might advise that "the invalid" was to be conducted from his bedroom to a couch in the parlor whereon Nicholls might get an instantaneous view of the transit—the sick man unidentifiable from having neglected to shave for several days and from his unique nightcap and other clothing. But since there was only one such sort of man at Longwood—obviously this was Napoleon.

Montholon was becoming increasingly urged in two diverse paths—the first involving the protection of his charge in his need for privacy, the second a wish to appear helpful to the British, since he was engaged in a program of improving his relations with Lowe to the end that that official might eventually exert influence on his behalf to effect his return to France. Accordingly he became more helpful in arranging many of these "sightings," being at the same

EXITS AND AN ENTRANCE

time aware that the merest glimpse of a muffled shadow in a darkened room would make happy the frustrated soul of the orderly officer while revealing nothing of any value, yet filling that man with gratitude to the count for his complaisance and aid in what was really a most unseemly business.

It is certain that neither Nicholls nor any of his successors in office ever positively identified the object of their earnest daily search, or knew him to be the actual ex-Emperor of the French in person. The man they did see, however, without doubt looked somewhat reminiscent of the Napoleon of countless drawings and paintings, but grown gross and awkward as one might expect in a man reported to take no exercise, to be continually sunk in depression—and become, moreover, careless as to toilet and clothing. Of course this individual had to be Napoleon—who else could it have been, in the name of common sense?

No one, it must be repeated, who had ever seen or known Napoleon prior to 1818 was ever permitted to look on the living prisoner again, and there was to be but one visitor, one only, admitted to his presence after that year—whereas before then there had been dozens and scores—prominent personages, world travelers, famous soldiers and influential people of many professions. A consideration of this occasion on which arrived the one visitor Longwood was to receive after 1818 is bound to be interesting and informative.

Early in 1819 the French learned of the arrival in Jamestown of a Mr. Charles Ricketts who was a cousin of Lord Liverpool, the British Prime Minister, and an influential Tory. Here was a unique opportunity for the exiles to state their case to one who, if sympathetic, might well be able to exert influence at the very fountainhead of British policy, on his return to England—perhaps effecting their removal to a more tolerable location or in some

WHO LIES HERE?

manner alleviating their condition and prospects. It was an opportunity not likely to be repeated, a way of bypassing Hudson Lowe and of having their pleas presented in the only quarter having the actual power to reprove or undo altogether that threatening and repressive figure.

Here it is essential to keep in mind the fact that the French household, now more than ever before, were feeling the need to do something about shortening the term of their complex situation—by any maneuver or process possible for them—before existence in Longwood should become utterly intolerable. Even though their man might not be ready for such a confrontation, they agreed that the risk had to be taken. Ricketts, they heard, was to be in St. Helena only briefly, breaking his voyage from Calcutta to England with but a few days rest. Longwood, for the first time, took the initiative, and an invitation in Napoleon's name was sent by the Grand Marshal requesting the young man to call. In spite of Lowe's anticipated interference, it was accepted. In this instance the governor was not so ill-advised as to raise any insuperable objections, nor did he appear to regard it as improper that a visitor to Napoleon should be introduced at Longwood merely by Bertrand, and not by his august self as had been his original custom before the break in relations.

The appointment had been made two days in advance, and the Englishman acknowledged it formally. He was too well bred to comment, even in the privacy of his diary, on his host's extraordinary lack of preparation for an interview thus arranged with ample notice. He tells of being admitted to a small bedroom (he had been forewarned that the Emperor was ill), and that he could at first perceive nothing but a figure lying on the famed iron camp bedstead partly shrouded with its dark green drapes. The only light came from a single candle set in a lantern wrapped about with

EXITS AND AN ENTRANCE

a sheet of paper, but as his eyes adjusted to the gloom he was able to make out that the figure was garbed in a shirt only, and had a colored bandana handkerchief bound around the head; the face was adorned with "a three or four day growth of beard."

Truly, a strange way to choose for impressing an influential visitor; perhaps, though, the latter's sympathies might have been expected to be enlisted thereby. But even in a much debilitated Napoleon, it would have been greatly out of character. Four days unshaven? With two valets in residence? Not to speak of the bandana around the head—all of this sounds much more like a deliberately assumed disguise, one which might be excused by the guest as appropriate to the peculiar circumstances: illness, depression, ennui, the environment.

The points made during this interview are of no concern, not being germane to our inquiry—they were the stock arguments that the Emperor had so often presented in the past both in his local expostulations and in the copious flow of written material sent forth by illicit means around the world. No doubt Bertrand, who was present during the session and who interjected remarks from time to time when it appeared that his principal required priming, had well rehearsed all this matter with the "invalid" during the preceding days. Although Lowe had forewarned Ricketts that Napoleon's style of speech would be harsh and roughly abrupt, the young man noted that his host's sentences were, on the contrary, "well turned" and his voice smoothly modulated. In addition he appeared to be "a little deaf," and at times tended to drift off into incoherency.

Unfortunately for the hopes of the household the young aristocrat, who at this time appeared to them to be encouragingly sympathetic, belonged to another world entirely—that of the Establishment, of course—and his report in London was to be cool

WHO LIES HERE?

and indifferent. The results of the interview, so desperately undertaken, were nil.

That well-staged event, however, provides much that is instructive. It should be kept in mind that Ricketts had never before seen the Emperor. How about the innumerable paintings, etchings, and miniatures whereby anyone of the time might be presumed to have been familiar with the Imperial features and countenance? Of all these it has been truly remarked that no two of them are alike, that often enough they seem to depict entirely different men —while in none of them is the subject portrayed with whiskers, or with a bandana for a headpiece.

Of those few who had known Napoleon or had had access to Longwood in the past, all were gone: Lowe and his staff (the latter made up of men all unfamiliar with the Imperial visage in the flesh) were one and all debarred from the presence, even from the near environs. The Balcombe family was gone, and Dr. O'Meara also; none of the doctors who were, later on, to be permitted to assist in the examination of the now seriously ailing prisoner had ever seen their patient before—although there can be no doubt but that all men carried with them something of a preformed image of so widely famed a personage. Into this general mental picture there is reason to believe that the Longwood tenant was most certainly able to fit himself—as the comment of the innumerable viewers of his corpse attests. It cannot be too often stated however, that given a moderate degree of resemblance in a substitution that notorious hat and costume would be the clinchers. They were then, yet are, and ever will be the trademark of the genuine. Napoleon in a top hat, a business suit with long trousers? He had assumed this style of garb on numerous occasions in the past—a "round hat" they called it then, and pantaloons—and one might well believe it to have been the only disguise he ever would have required, so

EXITS AND AN ENTRANCE

unlikely and unnatural it would have appeared to any suspicious scrutiny, to one prepossessed by that total image so well and so long publicized, known around the world.

The Ricketts interview had been in the spring. In July of the same year Captain Nicholls was reporting a typical tale of woe and exasperation: "Yesterday I was on my feet for at least *ten hours* walking about Longwood garden, but had no opportunity of seeing Bonaparte. The weather at present is so very bad that I fear my health will be greatly injured." This sort of fate pursued the unlucky man day after day, until at last the good-natured Bertrand suggested that he look in through the open bathroom window where "I saw General Bonaparte up to his neck in steaming water of his bath—he had a most ghastly appearance."

In August Lowe himself was able to report a sighting, made from horseback as he rode by the grounds: "I had on August fourth a most distinct view of his person. He had his back turned towards me. . . ." These were surely typical sightings, one might remark—and so rare had even such as these become that there appears a sort of gratified excitement glowing through the written accounts of them. Little wonder, in view of the driving anxiety of the watchers, that they appeared only too willing to persuade themselves that the brief visions infrequently vouchsafed them —always under adverse or impossible viewing conditions—had been veritable and veracious "sightings" of the Emperor himself. Nevertheless, in Lowe's communications with Bathurst during the remainder of this period, his increasing sense of insecurity and the gnawing uncertainty that plagued the man as to his prisoner's actual presence shows through in many places: He seems to have been the only man on the island who, at times at least, was capable of imagining just what might be the true situation up there on the foggy hill. Little wonder that his fingernails were gnawed to the

WHO LIES HERE?

quick, that he developed nervous tics and maddened his secretaries by his increasingly vile moods and irrational domination.

The question may be asked—and was asked: If there is all this uncertainty, if the prisoner refuses to admit the orderly officer or an official from Plantation House who can really verify his presence, as should be done regularly—why not force an entrance, even into his bedroom? Who does this impotent fellow think he is that we may be hoodwinked and put off in this matter? We have the force—let's use it and let him see we can no longer be bluffed!

The reason it was never attempted was twofold. First, Napoleon had from the beginning announced his determination, should anyone attempt to burst into his private quarters at any time, to retaliate in the same manner: by the use of force. To this end he kept two loaded pistols at his bedside, showing them to O'Meara in order that Lowe should be made aware of the exact situation, telling the doctor as well as all others that he would fire instantly at any intruder. The potential intruders believed him implicitly, and the private quarters were never broached. Not because of any lack of will to do so—Sir Thomas Reade often urged such measures as the boring of holes in the bedroom ceiling, so that Bonaparte might be kept under scrutiny night and day; the Marquis de Montchenu—as unwarlike a little man as could be conceived—urged that he be given a company of grenadiers, with whom he would soon effect an entrance into the forbidden precinct. Lowe, however, felt himself prevented from these courses by a consideration not affecting his advisers.

This was public opinion. All were aware of the rising tides of discontent in England and Europe—strikes, cavalry used to restrain unarmed mill workers, hunger and spreading deprivation among the middle and lower classes, a blight of unemployment and ruined industries—while the rich continued blissfully to enjoy the rewards of speculation and favoritism at corrupt courts. It had

EXITS AND AN ENTRANCE

not been this way—at least it had not seemed to be—under Napoleon's rule. As the months passed those days seemed better days, his memory more wonderful and solacing. Their ears—the ears of the dispossessed, of the inglorious poor—were attuned to news, any news, from the distant island where another race of oligarchs joined with their own to oppress their idol, to humiliate and torture him. They all knew the details, they had been told of the pistols at the bedside, the threats of invasion of their old Emperor's last shred of privacy. In the touchy condition of London and Paris and the major industrial cities, news of this last act of brutal repression would have been, in all probability, the spark in a powder keg.

No one would have liked better to confront Napoleon by force than Hudson Lowe—none felt a greater need to do so—yet he realized he would in all probability be writing *finis* to his career by the act, and he refrained.

The falling away of the Longwood staff was at first gratifying to the governor—it enabled him to effect economies in the catering costs, for one thing; there would be a lesser number of potential conspirators to be guarded against, and a thinner wall of personnel between the elusive prisoner and those set to guard him. It was also a source of some vindictive pleasure to realize that this once-mighty man was, like himself, fallible and vulnerable—his servants deserted him and two of his officers had found themselves unable to tolerate his proximity for very long. Let the process continue and at last the arrogant fellow would be compelled to give up his pose of exclusiveness and disdain, would no doubt come begging for Lowe's favors and personal consideration—as he should have done from the beginning.

True enough, within Longwood the apparent desertions tended to strike at the solidarity of the front the French attempted to maintain in a foreign citadel and became the focus of an increas-

WHO LIES HERE?

ingly disturbing reflection for them all as the concept struck home: All that is keeping us together now, the only factor holding us here any longer, is the need for the money that has been promised us for our continued loyalty—if we stay on to the end!

The truest friendship the prisoner was to form at Longwood was with one of the humbler members of the staff: the kindly and faithful valet, Marchand: a man with whom he could converse plainly, could unburden himself. When all the others had gone, he told Marchand, there would remain but the two of them, and at the last the younger man could close his eyes and then go back to his home in France. There can be no question as to the valet's affectionate loyalty, his infinite patience and endurance as his duties became increasingly harassing and onerous. That he had been intimately involved in the conspiracy to effect Napoleon's removal from the island is beyond any doubt, since his role thereafter would necessarily be one of the most intimate and demanding. That he was worthy of the great trust the Emperor had reposed in him is equally apparent: He was to be rewarded well for his virtue, standing second only to Montholon in terms of the endowment defined in his master's will. Because in this document Napoleon had referred to him, perhaps inadvertently, as "Count," this title was eventually conferred on him by his country, by then grown more fully conscious of the glorious period in which he had served so obscurely and so indispensably.

Bertrand has an interesting entry for the beginning of the new year of 1819. Napoleon had been, through nearly all of his adult career, a habitual user of snuff. It was supplied to him on St. Helena by the pound. A word portrait of the Emperor would have been incomplete without some reference to his continual snuff-taking, to the mannerisms in which most of it was wasted by

EXITS AND AN ENTRANCE

spillage, then flicked away in a cloud from the front of his waistcoat.

There would be no more of this. General Bertrand announced that Napoleon had discarded the habit and would require no more snuff.

The changes were beginning to appear.

Part Three
TOKENS AND TESTAMENTS

> *Look here upon this picture—and on this,*
> *The counterfeit presentment.* . . .
> —SHAKESPEARE

> *We made a tremendous mistake in getting rid of Napoleon. He is the man we ought to have had!*
> —WELLINGTON

There HAS been in existence, since the days when the news of Napoleon's death was first blown northward to the ears of strangely disturbed Europeans, by then grown somewhat forgetful of the Empire and its grandeurs, a sort of folk legend, widespread and widely believed: that the dead man in his remote grave was not the Emperor but another who had been substituted for him; that the real Emperor was yet alive, withdrawn from the active world and his imperial ambitions; that the British had been, after all, thoroughly deluded and humbugged by the Corsican king-master.

Even today the story has much of its original vitality and is from time to time republished—gaining, one suspects, a trifle in detail or circumstance at each reappearance. Nevertheless it carries with it many of the ostensible earmarks of authenticity, and its persistence over the years may be partly attributed to its intriguing aura of plausibility, its semblance of historicity. Ultimately, when one feels himself impelled to give an accounting for the strange post-1818 phenomena of Longwood, this is the narrative and this alone that at once leaps to the mind; it is the only one of several crudely devised versions that bears with it the cachet of truth.

It may very well be true—there is no reason why it could not be. I believe that it is.

WHO LIES HERE?

The story relates that in March of the year 1808, the Emperor Napoleon commissioned his minister of police Fouché with the task of discovering an adequate double for himself, someone capable of impersonating him, of making routine appearances for him in private or in public—on boring occasions, perhaps, or even dangerous ones, when the placing of infernal machines or the presence of assassins might be anticipated. It would need to be a man sufficiently resembling him in form and feature as to create a successful illusion of his actual presence, at least when viewed from a moderate distance. It would not be the first time in history by any manner of means, that a monarch or other illustrious personage had employed such a method of deception in the interests of his own protection or convenience.

Fouché delegated this important task to a trusted subordinate named LeDru, and in this agent's memoirs, published in Liège in 1840, he recounts the tale of how he at last discovered a most suitable candidate through the cooperation of an intelligent officer of the Third Regiment of Voltigeurs—a Colonel de Rochalve, who had long noted the strong resemblance between one of his men and his Emperor. The name of this light infantryman was Eugène François Robeaud, and he was to be passed through the hands of LeDru to those of Fouché and thence to the presence of Napoleon—undergoing an intense police scrutiny at each stage.

The Emperor is reported as having been well pleased with the appearance, as well as with the abilities, of Robeaud, who is described as resembling his master "feature by feature." LeDru further accounts for him as having, after Waterloo's disaster, returned to his birthplace—the tiny hamlet of Baleicourt on the Meuse, where he lived with his widowed sister and her son, assisting them in the operation of a small farm. In the early spring of 1818, however, the town clerk of Baleicourt—a fervid royalist—reported to the police that all three members of this

TOKENS AND TESTAMENTS

family had disappeared from the village; their little property was deserted and apparently abandoned. A casual search was thereupon launched by the police ministry and after some months the sister was discovered living in Tours—some versions say it was in Nantes that she was found. Her circumstances appeared to be comfortable. She offered no real reason for the departure from Baleicourt. Her brother had gone away. Where had he gone? He had become a sailor and was presently on a voyage—on a long voyage. She had had a pension left her, she explained—for her attention had been drawn to the fact that she was maintaining a style of living not at all consonant with her previous condition. Eventually, it is recorded, her son was to become a magistrate, but his uncle was never seen again in France. At last the police gave up the case in frustration.

Years later someone reported that he had taken the trouble to look up Robeaud's name in Baleicourt's records of vital statistics of the period. It read: "Robeaud, Eugène François: born July nineteenth 1781, in this village. Died in St. Helena on————." The date had been deliberately obliterated.

In the St. Helena records there is no mention of the presence or the death of anyone named Robeaud during the period of Longwood's occupance by the French—or at any other acceptable period.

That is all of the tale regarding Robeaud, the Emperor's image. But that offers only half of the story—there is yet another portion, of equal interest at the least, left unexplained: What then happened to Napoleon?

The story goes on, in the same circumstantial manner, to tell that later in the year 1818 a French traveler calling himself Revard arrived in the city of Verona, where he met a man named Petrucci, who was by craft an optician but who in addition carried on a trade in diamonds and other precious stones. Revard eventually bought a share in this man's business, although it was said of him that he knew not a thing of affairs and cared less—for he appeared to be well supplied with money. Because of a marked resemblance he bore to the fallen Emperor of the French, the people of the neighborhood jokingly referred to him as "Napoleon." They judged him to be about fifty years of age, and he was regarded by all who knew him as a highly intelligent and well-informed man.

On August 23, 1823, a message came for Revard, who at once ordered a coach and prepared himself for departure, seeming to Petrucci to be much disturbed by the news he had received. He left a sealed envelope with his partner, requesting that if he had not returned within three months the envelope be forwarded to the King of France: He was going on a long journey, he explained, and "the times were evil."

At that time the Duke of Reichstadt (so styled by the Austrian Emperor, his grandfather, who wished to efface from the boy's mind all memory of his origins and earlier title) lay in Schönbrunn Castle in serious condition from a bout of scarlet fever. He was, of course, Napoleon's son by Marie Louise and from birth had been known as the King of Rome. On the night of September 5, twelve days after Revard had left Verona, one of the sentries on duty in the castle grounds spotted an intruder emerging from the ivy that draped a wall. He fired promptly, and the man dropped, fatally wounded. Before he expired, he was reported to have muttered some half-intelligible words: "Duke of Reichstadt . . . king . . . son . . ."

The dead man carried no papers, but his appearance so startled the military authorities that the French Ambassador was brought to view the body. So perturbed was he that he attempted to claim the body, but Marie Louise herself intervened and eventually it was interred in an unmarked grave at Schönbrunn—and all further mention of what could have become a serious international scandal was hushed up.

In due course Petrucci forwarded the sealed letter, and not long afterward was visited by French authorities. His sworn silence was purchased for the quite considerable sum of 100,000 crowns. However, thirty years later, in the year 1853, believing that by then he had waited a sufficient length of time, he revealed his story to the local police, asserting his conviction that his vanished partner had been none other than Napoleon Bonaparte.

That is the essence of the story. It varies, in its successive incarnations, on some of the minor details: Robeaud is sometimes spelled Roberaud or Robaud; his sister was discovered living in either Nantes or Tours; the exact date of his birth is a trifle inconsistent. The facts and figures quoted here are those of a distinguished French official whose account is preferable to others because of the wealth of detail he offers and because of his ready access to Baleicourt records.

It can be readily perceived that the narrative is both plausible and well supported: This, one feels instinctively, is how it must have been. There are not a few other fabricated fables regarding Napoleonic escapes from St. Helena—all of them of too frivolous a nature, or too crudely conceived, to deserve any consideration. Nevertheless, the common factor of interest in all of them is that people had realized that—if Napoleon had in fact escaped—of necessity he must have provided himself with a double to leave behind for the satisfaction of the British. The story of Robeaud —circumstantial, not improbable, amply detailed—is still the only one in the genre that is acceptable, for the others have none of these virtues and are unworthy of a moment's consideration save for that theme they all possess, which testifies to the public acceptance of the doctrine that there had been a duplicate "Emperor" employed.

These legends have appeared often during the last thirty years or so in books, essays and articles. The magazine *Coronet,* for example, carried in its November, 1937, issue a lengthy investigation by Pierre Artige of the Robeaud material, together with accounts of several similar stories that had at one time or another caught the public interest. Most of the latter include fantastic accounts of the liberated Napoleon's subsequent activities and exploits. Frank Edwards, too, in one of his popular collections of accounts of strange phenomena, has offered an enhanced version.

There is a most readable account contained in a lengthy footnote in Dame Mabel Brookes' *Saint Helena Story,* while McCartney and Dorrance in their *Bonapartes in America* have done a fine job of research into the nature of the several escape plots known to have been launched, in addition to another retelling of the Robeaud story. Finally, Thomas Costain was so intrigued by the tale that he wove it, in somewhat modified form, into the substance of his novel of St. Helena, *The Last Love.*

None of these, however, has concerned itself with showing the *necessity* for entertaining such a thesis, if the unlikely and inexplicable events after 1818 are to be rendered meaningful. For such writers to speculate on the possibility of an escape from St. Helena and to work out a *modus operandi* for it, showing how it *could* have been effected, is to have avoided from the beginning any consideration of the mass of evidence that infallibly points toward the need to recognize that an escape was, in actual fact, carried out—and successfully. They put the cart before the horse—and then leave the horse out of it altogether. First comes the evidence, from the official records; after that, the escape having become a foregone conclusion, the means employed may then be appropriately

TOKENS AND TESTAMENTS

analyzed. First things first—and now that we have a better idea of the possible identity of Napoleon's successor in Longwood, it will be easier to look at the evidence with a more comprehending eye.

In January of 1819 a ship's surgeon, Dr. John Stokoe, was called to Longwood by Lowe to attend his prisoner. Since he had the temerity to bring in a diagnosis of hepatitis (which was admittedly endemic on the island, the cause of innumerable deaths in the fleet and garrison), he was violently assailed by Lowe, who ordered him sent back to England in disgrace. No sooner arrived there than the Lords of the Admiralty, cooperating with Lowe, commanded that he be at once sent back to Jamestown to face a court-martial. There he received a bullying and grossly unfair trial, was ordered dismissed from the service and once more sent back to England—a ruined man. A severe penalty this, and a lesson for any succeeding candidate for the office of Napoleon's physician to keep well in mind. It was not in the interests of either Lowe or his government to permit any rumor of the unhealthfulness of St. Helena to gain currency: This would have been to play directly into the hands of the local French, who were already spreading across Europe stories of the dampness, the rats, and the insalubrity of St. Helena and of Longwood in particular. It will be recalled that Dr. O'Meara had originally fallen foul of Hudson Lowe over his insistence on a similar diagnosis of liver ailment.

As a result of this affair, there was to be no doctor at Longwood for another nine months.

The little party that finally reached Longwood in September —sent out in sublime indifference by Madame Mère so long before, well aware that her son was no longer confined on the island—included the man who would be described through the years as Napoleon's last physician. He was usually accorded the courtesy title of Doctor, although he had not the least pretension to it in actuality, being but an anatomist's assistant. He was early compelled to admit to his patient that "up to the present I have had only corpses to deal with." There can be no question, however, of his qualifications as a dissector: They were well recognized, and as such he was readily granted the leading role among the group of British doctors gathered for the final autopsy on May 6, 1821. But at the time of his arrival his uncouth manner and the evidence of his frightening incompetence as a physician—coupled with the gross unsuitability of the two priests and the new servants—were sufficient to inform the unfortunate prisoner that his fate was a matter of unconcern to all involved—from the British ministry down to the humblest of the Longwood "service"—that in fact all of these might well have sound reasons for wishing for his speedy demise. With sturdy common sense he set about devising a regime for himself designed to delay their hopes for as long as possible.

According to Antommarchi, he himself was instrumental in inspiring in his patient an inclination toward new outside interests, such as would provide the open-air exercise of which the prisoner had long deprived himself by remaining immured within the buildings. Soon thereafter the "General" was to be seen by the wondering British observers to have become an enthusiastic devotee of gardening! He arose daily long before the remainder of the household, and by swinging a large bell he roused up the reluctant personnel to come out and join him in his labors: the officers, the priests, the doctor, the servants and the children—they all pitched in and toiled with a will. Many varieties of flowers and plants were set out, a sunken garden was created, and twenty-four large willows, as well as orange and peach trees and many oaks, were set about it. Hudson Lowe now appeared only too glad to cooperate in these projects, contributing a number of trees and shrubs from the Cape; at last he had seen the unpleasant truth for himself that for him alone, among the ranks of the British personnel, Napoleon's

TOKENS AND TESTAMENTS

death would bring at the very least a drastic reduction in his income and mode of living. Here his position was exalted, his income and living allowances extraordinarily high, and his daily life that of an English country gentleman of wealth. And all this would inevitably cease should the reason for his presence be taken by death. It seems strange that the governor had not realized all this long before.

A new access of life and vitality, manifesting itself in strange and unlikely ways—in ways inappropriate, indeed, and in glaring contrast to the previously displayed tastes and habits of the Emperor!

The Jamestown plumber built a sunken pond for Longwood gardens—a tank twelve feet in length. One fine March day in the year 1820 (in the southern hemisphere, the height of summer) the lookouts on adjacent hills might have been much edified at the spectacle of their plump captive peeling off his clothes, in the presence of the servants, to plunge himself into the refreshing coolness of the pond.

All these things were of course retailed to Lord Bathurst in London, with emphasis on a particular account of the General having been observed building a sod wall around his sunken garden—thereby ensuring to himself some partial immunity, at the least, to supervision by his captors when he wished to walk in his grounds; some protection, too, from the steady, wearing blast of the southeast trades. He had been seen receiving the sods into his own hands, then pushing and pressing them into alignment. Suddenly one realizes, with a degree of astonishment, how very far the man must have deviated by this period—digging in the harsh soil, handling masses of dirt, planting and transplanting, creating walls of sod, actually wielding shovel and hoe! All this would have been natural and proper to the peasant Robeaud, of course—but to

WHO LIES HERE?

the Emperor of the French? He, so vain of his delicate and womanish hands? Quite inconceivable!

Almost as inconceivable, moreover, was the costume first adopted by the General at this time: loose-fitting and shapeless pantaloons bought for him in Jamestown; a common jacket, a wide-brimmed straw hat. All very sensible under the circumstances, no doubt, but a far cry from the prestigious uniforms, the Imperial manner and presence. The uniform was still worn, however, in the cooler weather and at mealtimes, in order that the watchers might be reassured and the morale of Longwood be maintained—at least superficially.

Clouds were gathering, however. As all gardeners soon discover, their labors present an irresistible temptation to bird and beast—and the depredations of these invite a drastic response in the outraged breasts of Adam's heirs. Longwood's new plantings were not long spared the common menace—the inroads made by the wandering animal life of the plateau—and the General responded instantly in the manner of any suburban gardener similarly threatened: He lost his temper and ran for his firearms. Some of the goats kept by Madame Bertrand were the first to attempt pillage, and one of them was mercilessly slain by a charge of ball from the General's carbine. Three hens and yet another goat, all belonging to the groom Archambault, were the next to be martyred, to be followed by the three hens of the Swiss, Noverraz, a servant. The last sacrifice to the gardens was one of two oxen belonging to the East India Company, and the wounding of his fellow-criminal.

These bloody deeds were not performed with immunity, however, and the current orderly officer, a Captain Lutyens, expostulated vigorously to Montholon over the inherent danger to possible bystanders; as a matter of fact this very point became a matter of serious consideration in correspondence between Lowe and

TOKENS AND TESTAMENTS

Bathurst. The governor wished to be advised as to the legal position in which Bonaparte would be placed should he, accidentally or designedly, commit a murder—or even mayhem only—in this fashion? It was too much for the ministry, and the point appears never to have been settled.

All this disturbance was as nothing, however, compared with the violent reaction of the Swiss valet Noverraz to the loss of his hens. He had been a man notoriously faithful, having served Napoleon in the Tuileries since 1809, following him through all his trials and reverses. Now he went instantly to Plantation House and laid his complaint before the governor—denouncing General Bonaparte furiously and demanding that he be permitted to leave the island at once. Once again Lowe may have considered it in his own best interests to take the part of the prisoner—the man was now no trouble at all, had become quiet and docile, engaged in generally harmless pursuits: Why stir him up again by depriving him of an old and trusted servant? He was successful in placating Noverraz and in inducing him to return peaceably to Longwood—where he did in fact stay on, until the very end.

Here, yet once again, is behavior strikingly at variance with that to be anticipated from the world's greatest soldier; a man ever conscious, moreover, of the appearances and of the effect of his actions and manner on others—above all things aware of the need to maintain the imperial dignity and to do and say the appropriate thing. The potting of barnyard animals and tame creatures is hardly consonant with the poise and even serenity the fallen monarch had maintained—during his first three years of captivity—in the face of countless thwartings and humiliations. And yet again—it is the sort of behavior one might more readily believe in a man of Robeaud's background.

That for the loss of three hens an old and loyal intimate servant should show such instant spleen, such an open contempt for his master as to betray the whole deplorable business to Sir Hudson, requesting his own repatriation, is difficult to comprehend. It might have been, however, a manifestation of the general indifference and even disrespect notably on the increase during the prisoner's last years of life.

Antommarchi, for instance, was careless and even insolent almost from the beginning of his tenure, having had to be reproved more than once for appearing before his patient casually clothed, or even in partial undress. He was corrected sharply for presuming to refer to Counts Montholon and Bertrand by their surnames only—as though contemptuous of the farce he was expected to participate in; he would grin, silently and sneeringly, at his patient when the latter made some simple allusion to religious matters. Whenever he felt the need to seek out female solace—a constant preoccupation with him, apparently—he would ride off to Jamestown even on the invalid's worst days, staying away overnight whenever he chose to, with never a word of explanation. Many times, toward the end, messengers were sent galloping to the town to attempt to locate him and bring him to his master's relief.

General Bertrand, too—he, the Gibraltar in this dwindling group of exiles—was exhibiting an increasing indifference to the amenities and to the expression of the deference to be expected of him as Grand Marshal of the Palace. This negligence was observed by the relays of watchers, who reported on the many days when he neglected to go to dinner at Longwood, for example, preferring to dine at home with his family. As for Madame Bertrand, there appeared to be a feud that prevented her visiting the General at all; she came, at last, when he was on his deathbed. Even Montholon felt obliged to include mention of this behavior in his diary, since he knew that the whole island had been made aware of it: He wrote that "he [Bertrand] presents himself at a fixed hour, appearing not

TOKENS AND TESTAMENTS

to care particularly whether he is or is not received—and Madame B. is not seen at Longwood for months at a time." Such a statement would have been inconceivable of the tightly knit court of pre-1818! Finally, both Bertrand and his lady openly declared their unwillingness to remain longer on the island and asked Montholon to obtain permission for their departure. The incredible had come to pass!

Then Antommarchi, chafing under his reprimands and resenting the general atmosphere of disapproval, asked to be sent home. Shortly there would be none of the official group left save Montholon—and he was sending incessant instructions to his wife, urging her to obtain a substitute for himself at the earliest possible moment. On October 4, 1820, Gentilini, a loyal Elban footman, took his departure. His application had been hanging fire for months, during which time he had wept almost continually, in deep depression.

In January of 1821 the now swiftly failing invalid was forced to request, through Montholon, a new doctor and another priest, for the old Abbé Buonavita had at last expressed his need to go away. The ailing man's one stipulation as to the qualifications of the two men to be sent out to him might be thought something curious: It was that "no member of my family be consulted as to the choice." The doomed Robeaud had realized, of course, from the wretched selection that had been dispatched for ultimate arrival on September 20 of 1819 that the Bonaparte family was fully apprised of the situation at Longwood. By inviting the aid of strangers and sympathizers he stood a better chance, he must have recognized, of obtaining people at least partly qualified to fill the two positions.

And how does orthodox history explain that pathetically revealing request of the dying man they call Napoleon—that no member of his family be consulted as to the choice of his doctor and priest? I have found no comment on it. No doubt it would be impossible to

WHO LIES HERE?

explain except by the thesis of madness, as in the case of Madame Mère and her conviction that Napoleon was nearing Malta. Perhaps the dying man was subject to delusions of persecution —everyone was attempting to kill him, by acts either of commission or of omission? No, this has not been directly stated—the peculiar provision is generally ignored, or blamed on Napoleon's distrust of his own family. However, we have plenty of evidence that he did trust, and had every reason to trust, at least three of them—his mother above all, his sister Pauline Borghese, and his son-in-law Eugène, all of them in Italy. One cannot help but regard that desperate proviso as a cry from the heart of the doomed substitute who realized that everyone's hand was against him, his death their impatiently awaited release. Otherwise it is inexplicable.

From that time on the symptoms of the decline became so pronounced that it was evident to all that the invalid's life could not long persist. Accordingly the Bertrands made up their minds to stay on to the end, as did both Montholon and Antommarchi. By that time the old priest, Buonavita, and the footman, Gentilini, were already gone.

The last Longwood incident to be observed by the British took place in 1820, after the garden had been finished but not yet shielded by the sod wall: Lord Charles Somerset, the governor of the Cape of Good Hope, was en route to England accompanied by his two daughters, and since his ship required to go into St. Helena for water, he decided to take advantage of the opportunity to pay a visit to Napoleon. Through Lowe he sent the customary request for permission to call—but there was no response from Montholon. In spite of this rebuff Lord Charles and the two young ladies decided to go sightseeing anyway, feigning an interest in the new house then being constructed for Napoleon at Longwood, but no doubt

TOKENS AND TESTAMENTS

hoping they might have the good fortune to sight the Emperor in his grounds. Captain Lutyens, the orderly officer, later reported to Major Gorrequer at Plantation House that "Bonaparte was at dinner in the garden under the oak trees, with Count Montholon. Lord Charles and the young ladies passed round the garden into the wood. As soon as they were perceived, the General rose from his dinner and *ran* into the house. The dinner was carried in after him. After Lord Charles' party had left Longwood, General Bonaparte immediately came out."

There had been, of course, no rudeness in his act—the rudeness was on the part of the people who so inconsiderately chose to invade the privacy of the captive's grounds, in spite of having been rebuffed so unmistakably. Yet this was that same man, presumably, possessed of that superb balance and control that never in a long public career had found itself unequal to the facing down of pope, monarch, priest or diplomat; the one who had dominated and bent to his will the emperors of Russia and Austria; he who had matched blades with such masters of effrontery and malice as Metternich and Talleyrand, and a horde of lesser rascals. This man, in whom a knowledge of his own superiority, of his genius, was bred in the bone, at the sight of a group of chattering tourists tosses poise and ordinary dignity to the winds, running grotesquely to shelter like any country bumpkin! One knows, as well as he knows what his own behavior in such circumstances would be, that the real Napoleon would either have yielded gracefully and sent to have the visitors called over to chat with them affably—or he would have turned his back resolutely and proceeded with his dinner unconcerned.

The instinctive reaction was that of a peasant or a private soldier rather than of an Emperor; there is no better test of a man's quality than his reaction to a situation startling or unexpected. The panicky dash for the house—so unnecessary, so hopelessly

WHO LIES HERE?

wrong—was the response of a Robeaud, not of a Napoleon. And this was but one of several such incidents reported in the years after 1818. They are, of course, reported by outside observers, those of the British who were witnesses, and not by the French diarists only; these latter, had they thought it possible to do, would doubtless have left such discreditable and revealing accounts out of their journals—yet dared not when they realized that other eyes and pens would infallibly record them and thus tend to expose their own witness to charges of bias or deletion of unfavorable details regarding their idol.

Too much to be inferred from so minor an incident? The incident is far from minor in its implication, and the inference is unavoidable. Many a would-be playwright has had his work disqualified for putting into his hero's mouth speeches such a man could not possibly have made; for making him perform in a manner wholly inappropriate to his carefully built-up background, his nature. This fundamental sort of error betrays the amateur. It appears that Robeaud was still an amateur when left for a few minutes unattended, or deprived temporarily of his prompters. He knew, even more than the others, that he was on increasingly shaky ground, and at times the knowledge must have been frightening indeed.

Most of the essentials of the story have been described and considered; it is time to recapitulate and to integrate what has been learned with what must be inferred, insofar as it is possible —always recalling that the actors in such a hazardous enterprise are not likely to leave blueprints behind for our instruction. Very soon after the *Northumberland* left England with its freight of exiles, Parliament enacted laws providing penalties inclusive of death for participation in an escape of the prisoner from St.

TOKENS AND TESTAMENTS

Helena, and for the least complicity, long terms of imprisonment. So lively was the apprehension inspired in the French by their awareness of this law and its provisions that it is evident that they went to extreme lengths to obliterate, conceal or destroy any record of their clandestine activities and manipulations. There was General Gourgaud's diary, or that part of it completed up to the time of his departure, much of which was phrased with an eye to its confiscation by Hudson Lowe—thus to reinforce in that suspicious individual's mind the already implanted beliefs regarding the violence of the general's hatred for his erstwhile Longwood companions, his long-festering aversion for all things Jacobinical. It was necessary that Lowe be convinced that these sentiments were of long standing, to destroy any suspicion that they might be insincere and only recently expressed: for this end there could be no better witness than the private journal, its sentiments entered over a long period of time, and dated. Artifices of this sort were demanded of the conspirators if their involvement were not to be discovered—their very lives might be endangered by the revelations of one man.

In this connection one's mouth is set to watering at the thought of the written treasure yet buried somewhere in Longwood's grounds—matter too dangerous even to dream of smuggling out when Lowe stood ready and prepared to scrutinize everything on paper owned by the departing Frenchmen! Since "Napoleon" was then safely dead and buried, with what fearsome business could it possibly have dealt? But we have the written word of the principals (set down in their respective journals long after the departure, of course) that these papers *were* buried: It is not a speculative affair. It seems probable that they are still there, in the hiding place selected for them in May of 1821, for certainly the French had no opportunity to unearth them before setting sail from St. Helena. Such a

WHO LIES HERE?

rash act might have made prisoners of them all, and on the very threshold of liberty—and what good end would have been served had they succeeded?

There would be another opportunity, for some of them at least, in the year 1840.

In that year King Louis Philippe, seeking some means of bolstering his fading popularity with the French commons, hit on the theme of restoring Napoleon's remains to the capital city, of reviving his recent glories thereby and restoring, hopefully, some of the waning prestige of the throne. England's permission was obtained and a frigate, the *Belle Poule,* under the command of the king's son the Prince de Joinville, set off for St. Helena. On board were Bertrand, Gourgaud and Marchand, as well as the young Las Cases, whose father was dead. Count Montholon had taken temporary shelter in England as the result of bankruptcy proceedings against him in Paris, so the old guard from Longwood was represented by the faithful three.

On October 15, dampened by a persistent fall of rain, these men looked again on the features of the man they had laid to rest some nineteen years before. All the reports agree that the body was in a state of almost perfect preservation—there was a little mildew on a polished jackboot, the gold braid was tarnished. There had been no attempt made to embalm the body, and yet there it lay, mocking by its youthfulness and beauty of countenance the aging men gathered about it. It was at once resealed into the original coffins, and the whole transferred to an enormously heavy and ornate sarcophagus that would enclose it forever within the red porphyry monument of Les Invalides.

The bemused comrades wandered about in their old haunts for several days—escorted everywhere, apparently, by the delighted officials of Jamestown; there had been very little of interest going

TOKENS AND TESTAMENTS

on in St. Helena since those extraordinary days of the Emperor's coming—and going. There was even a newspaper reporter in their group, and one can well imagine that no opportunity for solitude, let alone for digging aimlessly in the gardens of Longwood, would be given the French. At any rate, the activities, speeches and behavior of the group are set down in some detail.

Gourgaud, both on board the *Belle Poule* and on St. Helena, was much in evidence and obviously a privileged figure among the faithful—there was not the least sign of any lingering resentment or blame over his "treachery" of 1818! It is at this point that some professional historians have permitted themselves a moment of wonderment: at the presumptions implicit in his presence and total acceptance, after his brazen and fully recorded betrayal and perjury.

Actually, as some at least of his companions well realized, no man among them had a better right than he to be the honored witness of the removal of the body of this man—the man he had been chiefly instrumental in bringing there to this lonely grave, at the risk of his own life and repute. Even when they returned to France and the body was born through magnificently decorated streets to Les Invalides, the cheers of the great crowds were as loud for Gourgaud as for Bertrand and Marchand—they were all honored equally. But it is a virtual certainty that the party had not disinterred the secret documents, whatever they may have been, whose location and even existence was known to themselves alone.

To continue with the recapitulation: It has been shown how Napoleon from the first was determined to establish for himself a strict privacy at Longwood—an atmosphere impermeable to either curiosity or malicious interference—within which he was to be as safely ensconced as though the grounds had been sheathed in steel. Next was the creation of an effective intelligence bureau, of which the unfortunate Cipriani was the guiding genius, supplemented by the inconspicuous activities of every reliable member of the household.

After these things came the friendly enlistment of any and all cooperative or bribable souls into a private postal service, and the thorough testing of the reliability of this system by the dispatch to England, the Continent and perhaps America of many documents and parcels—the *Letters from the Cape,* for example, the *Answer to Lord Liverpool's Speech* and the *Manuscript of St. Helena* are among the best known of these.

When the first attempts were made to have Robeaud's whereabouts discovered, it is of course impossible to state; it must have very soon become evident to the plotters, however, that this long-range way of conducting so risky and uncertain a business would be impracticable: The average voyage between England and St. Helena was of fifty days duration—it had been seventy-one for the *Northumberland*'s voyage—which meant a total of almost four months elapsed between the sending of a letter and the receipt of an answer. To this intolerable delay was added the ever-present risk of loss or confiscation of the letters—perhaps the most crucial of a series—with consequent exposure of the principals and their ruin: ruin to those at Longwood as well as to those unnamed ones, the agents and friends willing to risk all for the cause. This way was the wrong one: It was absolutely necessary that someone of the household be sent, to act in person and on the scene.

The one to be sent must be a man thoroughly informed and primed to deal intelligently with every possible contingency that might arise; a man wholly loyal, quick-witted, resourceful and inventive, someone accustomed to organizing, commanding, improvising and executing. This could only be General Gourgaud. Las Cases had really been out of the question—too old, too transparent, wits too slow and formal, not able long to carry on a deception of this sort. His services were best utilized in the dissemination of favorable doctrine throughout the countries of western Europe.

Then followed the lengthy period devoted to the deception of Hudson Lowe and the other officials at Plantation House; here the young general's emotional nature and histrionic ability was to be of the greatest value—for he could and did burst into tears at a moment's notice, and thus had no difficulty in persuading the governor of the genuineness and thoroughness of his conversion, of his utter detestation of Napoleon and everyone at Longwood. After lengthy communications between Lowe and Lord Bathurst it was agreed that the renegade general should proceed forthwith to London, to make his revelations directly into the receptive ears of the British ministers themselves. As it turned out his papers, including the doctored diary, were only superficially inspected; he was not required to sail first to the Cape for such a quarantine as poor Las Cases had endured for eight months; and finally, when the *Campden* arrived in England he was whisked directly to London and interrogation.

No doubt due to the skeptical report of the French Commissioner Montchenu, Gourgaud was not to receive permission to enter France; Louis XVIII remained suspicious of this Napoleonic officer, and even in London there seemed to be an aura of polite dubiety. Gourgaud was quizzed repeatedly, the same ground being covered several times in obvious attempts to confuse or trap him. All during this time, and even later when it was apparent that France was going to be out of the question for him, he was reported as receiving and entertaining known Jacobins and radicals, as well as Bonapartists from the Continent.

There was nothing to prevent him from slipping away for a flying visit across the Channel at this time, for the British seemed temporarily to have lost interest in him and his not-so-spectacular revelations. As for the means—the narrow seas swarmed, as always, with small smuggling craft who would and did carry anyone for a price. Whether he did make such a trip is questionable, however, for discovery there meant for him arrest and a severe punishment. So dangerous a proceeding would hardly have been necessary in view of the fanatical devotion of a horde of Bonapartist adherents and partisans, and contact with merely one of these would at once put him into touch with a wide selection of potential agents.

First, there was money—a good deal of it—to be obtained from Napoleon's mother and her children at Rome; or there was Napoleon's son-in-law, Prince Eugène, who held a large sum in trust for the Emperor. While this was being arranged another expedition could set out for Baleicourt, the tiny hamlet lying a hundred and sixty miles to the northeast of Paris, to seek out the humble but vitally essential factor requisite to the success of the whole scheme.

There is still a fragment of the legend that bears on this matter of the search party, and for what it may be worth it can be included here. It relates that in June of 1818 a coach and four arrived in Baleicourt (and that would be a sufficiently rare phenomenon as to inspire remembrance!), the driver making inquiries as to the home of Eugène Robeaud. For the sake of curious neighbors the story was put about that this was just a physician who wished to buy some rabbits for a friend. It was not long after the coming of this coach that Robeaud and his two relatives were missed. Nor were they ever to be seen again in Baleicourt.

It is not in the least difficult to imagine the ex-rifleman-actor in the midst of this rural setting—he by now well disillusioned with the drab face of peacetime and weary of the dull round of toil that constituted his whole existence. He would seize hungrily at the proffer of a renewal of his old and brilliant role, not inquiring too

TOKENS AND TESTAMENTS

closely into the possible disadvantages or dangers of this remote, exotic theater. His old master needed him, had sent these men to find him across all those weary miles! Of course he was ready to play at being Emperor once again, for renown and reward. The French soldier of the time was an intense individualist, very much accustomed to dangers, very prone to yield to any appeals made in the name of *La Gloire* or *La Patrie* and which implied a reasonable chance of financial rewards. Like the rest of the old soldiers of the *Grand Armée*, Robeaud was still stunned by the disaster of Waterloo, by the collapse of the great empire and of all that had constituted their world for so long a time. If his Emperor was planning on returning yet once again to pull the wool over the eyes of the arrogant Bourbons, Prussians and English—should he not leap as of old to offer his aid, his unique talent?

If he had held back—at the first, say, owing to his shrewd distrust of sudden change or of bounty falling from the blue, so to speak—his sister would without doubt have promptly helped him to make up his mind: The persuasive visitor was speaking of unheard-of wealth to be acquired, with plenty of immediate money paid in hand as well. For her there was to be a town residence in the city of her choice, a good school for her son, an income for life—all this guaranteed in exchange for their total silence and cooperation: again it was stressed, it would be death for her brother and prison for herself should either of them ever breathe a word of the business Robeaud was to be engaged in or of what they had just been told.

What sort of a man might this Robeaud have been? It will be recalled that he had been taken from the ranks in 1808, a time when the Empire and Napoleon's fortunes were at their absolute zenith. The imperial stand-in was to be gradually introduced into aspects of magnificence—the glories of the Tuileries, the Elysée Bourbon, Fontainebleau, Malmaison and the other palaces and

WHO LIES HERE?

mansions. No doubt he must have received some heavy coaching for his role, possibly from Napoleon's friend, the actor Talma, who had coached the Emperor himself in regal posture and gesture when he first assumed the purple. After seven such years Robeaud must have attained to some degree of proficiency and authority in his part, perhaps developing a little of the matching temperament and spirit, something of the air and manner growing out of a psychic participation in the character he portrayed. Beyond doubt he must have practiced endlessly the Napoleonic scrawl and signatory initial, endorsing or receipting or negating in scores of minor instances as his master's confidence in him grew. Then he might be driven swiftly through the Paris streets, when Napoleon wished to impress on the citizenry his watchful presence in their midst, while he was preoccupied with private affairs or dallying with a current mistress.

He would have developed something of a natural dignity, perhaps, as long as he was supported by the others—those officers of the court who were aware of his existence and lent him their deferential cooperation. These courtiers, chamberlains, lackeys and all who were in on the secret would have been required to behave toward him with the courtesy and reverence they ordinarily offered the imperial figure—at least in public; and in private with ordinary civility, always. It would have been difficult for them to have done otherwise, so real was the illusion of the man's presence and manner, so suggestive of the actuality of the one before whom the world stood in awe. Besides all that, Robeaud was known to have access to the Emperor's privacy, as when he received instructions or rendered his report: The confidence thus expressed was calculated to inspire at least an elementary respect in the minds of those accustomed to watching how the wind blew, and trimming their sails thereby.

And daily—one may well believe it—the understudy would

TOKENS AND TESTAMENTS

return, thanks to his private gods, for the excellent fortune that had lifted him so amazingly out of the rough barrack-room atmosphere of his erstwhile comrades into the almost magnificent circumstances of his second life.

A man of origins so humble—quick, nevertheless, to learn, comprehending, not without imagination—would have enjoyed his work to the utmost and studied for continual improvement. Napoleon must have watched him too, in his turn, from time to time meditating on secret things: someday, someday . . . if all this should fail me, my star be obscured . . . some day that loyal instrument there . . . not allow him to disappear from my knowledge . . . a trump card in ultimate disaster, perhaps. But not at too close a range! Those eyes, dark brown . . . cursed shame . . . and four or more inches the less—can't have him always standing on a slab or be forever seated. . . . Well enough though, in spite of all . . . could be managed. . . .

The Emperor had created Robeaud. Because the man was grateful he was loyal, and because nature had made him so nearly a physical counterpart of the greatest man living, he revered him and would gladly have given his life for his idol.

The messenger who had called for Robeaud at the Baleicourt farmstead had of course been apprised of all these things and had played his cards skillfully and dynamically before both brother and sister, yet without stressing too soon the peculiar difficulties to be confronted in the situation awaiting the man at Saint Helena. What then?—at the very worst he would just live out his normal span of years there, as naturally but far more luxuriously than here on the gloomy Meuse; he would be master of a fine home stocked with excellent foods and wines—there would be many servants, the old familiar palace ways, titled officers to guide and support him. There would be no English, and no visitors admitted ever— all that had been seen to by the Emperor himself.

WHO LIES HERE?

In his turn Robeaud had, with peasant astuteness, left something unsaid on his own part; he refrained from speaking of the primary reason he had for taking up this messenger's offer. Physically he was no longer the man he had been, even though he was only thirty-seven. He found himself increasingly unable to stand up to a long day's work on the farm; there was sometimes an ugly pain like a knife twisting in his right side. Sometimes he felt it down in the groin, and then it might disappear for almost a month at a time. No use bothering with the doctors any longer—they knew so little and charged so much. But were he to die of all this—and who could say how soon that might be?—or to become bedridden and a burden on his sister, who would be there to handle the farm, or to save his sister and her boy from starvation?

If he kept silence about it, he would be betraying no one's hopes, after all, if he were in truth a doomed man; doubtless the people on the island would be relieved at his death, for then they could look forward to a return to their homes—while in the meanwhile he would have done a service for the man he loved, the great one who had rewarded him so well and whom he resembled so strangely.

His ears were active as he thought, and he listened attentively as the messenger repeated his instructions, making some notes the while in an almost illegible scrawl—one much like another the watching man remembered having seen before, in better days. Perhaps, he thought, after so many years of painstaking reproduction of the imperial scribble, the fellow could write in no other fashion. All so much to the good!

As for Robeaud fearing a double-cross—the possibility of a deliberate betrayal to the British of his deception—he was able to dismiss that anxiety after only a moment's reflection: These people had put themselves equally in his power. For, were he ever unmasked, the nations would at once learn that Napoleon was at

TOKENS AND TESTAMENTS

large and the world would be turned topsy-turvy until he was hunted down and dealt with. No, he could rely on perfect support—he was quite certain of that. And because the death-penalty would hang over his head always, as with them, they could trust him to the limit—even had his loyalty and financial interests been insufficient guarantees.

The sister, then, was sent to the city she had chosen, a trust was established to provide her with a pension, and a private school was found for her son. From this point on, Robeaud disappears, as far as the details of his long voyage and arrival on St. Helena are concerned—this is, of course, inevitable. The most convenient course would have been to establish him as a passenger, or even as a member of the crew, on a vessel of the East India Company—the only ships permitted to come into Jamestown harbor. And the most suitable ship would have been one trading from the Mediterranean to Rio de Janeiro, say—and way points. The company's ships retained the right to use St. Helena for watering or victualing or for repairs, and therefore their bottoms and those of the British Navy constituted the entire shipping of Jamestown harbor. In this connection it is of interest to read that the *David* sailed from St. Helena for Rio on August 22, 1818. If Robeaud had indeed accompanied her from Europe and had transferred himself from her decks to the privacy of Longwood, Napoleon might very well have replaced him aboard this ship. At any rate there was a certain influential personage who did embark, one who seemed to have had at least a faint inkling of what might have been going on. He has been dealt with before, but deserves a further accounting here.

The Count Alexander Balmain, as previously implied, stood head and shoulders above the other two commissioners as to diplomatic qualifications, background and personal characteristics; he had been approved for his post on St. Helena by the Russian Emperor himself, for the Czar continued to be impressed

WHO LIES HERE?

by the memory of the fallen monarch who had once been his personal friend, and whom he himself had befriended even after Elba, as has been pointed out. That he was still somewhat under the spell of that magic personality is evident from the implications of many of his observations and actions. There is every reason why he should have been, for Alexander was the kind of genial, semimystical man who was almost always under someone's influence—currently it was a weird woman known as Madame Krüdener, a clairvoyante and psychic counsellor, shriveled and minute in person but apparently able to dominate and direct other statesmen and ministers as well as Alexander. She was having a great European vogue at this period.

So the Russian Emperor continued to receive his private reports on Napoleon, and to read them avidly. It is hardly possible to believe, in the face of the evidence, that he wished him anything but well; he might even have offered his aid to his distressed onetime mentor—had the eyes of all his royal colleagues not been so intently fixed on him and on his every action. That he was hungry for any comment on Longwood and on its relations with Lowe, for example, is shown in the wording of many of the letters from the Russian minister to Balmain—encouraging him to become ever more discursive or explicit in his reports because of the marked pleasure they provided the Czar. Balmain had learned to despise Hudson Lowe from the beginning, and was scathing in his frequent caricaturing of the governor and his policies, of his pettifogging conduct toward the French exiles. The limitations of island society, however, coupled with a normal antipathy to a life of enforced celibacy, at last brought about an unforeseen rapprochement between these two unlikely principals: Count Balmain became violently smitten with the charms of Lowe's step-daughter Charlotte, and consequently was an increasingly more frequent visitor at the mansion; accordingly his later opinions of Sir Hudson were considerably modified—as to their active expression, at least. As a matter of interest he married the young lady in 1820, and a few days afterward he left St. Helena forever.

From the time of his arrival Balmain had made a most favorable impression on the French at Longwood, his repute being borne to them by gossip and the efforts of their intelligence group as well as by casual contacts made with him when out riding; from all this Napoleon was in turn led to think well of the commissioner, whom he nevertheless did not meet in person. Several attempts had been made to bring about an interview at Longwood (for the Emperor refused always to ride outside the grounds because of the indignity of having to be accompanied by a British officer, as per Lowe's regulation)—but to no avail: The watchfulness of the governor, mad with wild suspicions that even the most innocent of circumstances served to inflame, rendered the commissioners ultra-prudent after they had experienced a few irritating repercussions or humiliating interrogations. For this cause alone none of the three foreign representatives, all quite naturally eager to meet the great prisoner, were ever to have anything but a telescope view of him.

Yet, and in spite of the seeming indifference displayed by these gentlemen to approaches from Longwood, Napoleon (who was not unaware that they were being blackmailed, as it were, into their seeming indifference to meeting him) still retained a high hope that his onetime pupil and confederate Alexander would be persuaded to employ his very considerable influence on his behalf amidst the inimical rulers of Europe. He had at last come to realize the futility of expecting anything whatever from the English, nor any alleviation in the attitude of stony indifference adopted by his father-in-law, the Austrian Emperor; with Alexander, however—could contact have only been attained, even through his minister—there could be, he thought, a strong hope of goodwill to be enlisted.

WHO LIES HERE?

He was well aware of the pronounced visionary tendency in the Russian monarch, the bias toward mystic introspection, even to superstitious influences: It had been at the Czar's instigation that the European powers had been induced to collaborate under the name of the Holy Alliance—the baffled but overruled signatories affecting to subscribe, in this charter, to a list of vaguely Christian objectives that not one of that cynical and worldly crew could have privately countenanced for even a moment. By most of these Alexander was regarded as benignly mad, but—he possessed the biggest battalions, currently, as Napoleon had been wont to phrase such things; for the time being the ministries saw the wisdom of going along with the pretense of supporting Alexander's pious eccentricities.

Therefore, as the virtual dictator of Continental policy, had Alexander chosen to speak out before the sovereigns for amelioration of the rigors inflicted on their humbled prisoner, he could beyond any doubt have achieved his ends—short of actually setting Napoleon at liberty. It would have been regarded as yet another manifestation of the Czar's religious mania, to be responded to even as had been his "Holy Alliance"—a matter possibly equally controversial.

From the time of the celebrated Peace of Tilsit—where the two great Emperors had met on an ornate raft in midstream to divide Europe between themselves—Napoleon had brought the younger man under his hypnotic sway; thereafter Alexander's admiration for his genius had never wholly passed away. It was to persist, even in spite of the campaign of 1812 and the destructive occupancy of Moscow, through all the hostilities of the latter years of the empire. It had been principally through the Russian's influence that the terms of the Peace of Paris, dictated in 1814, won for Napoleon a fate much more lenient than the nations had been

TOKENS AND TESTAMENTS

prepared to enforce against the menacer of their ancient institutions.

It is true that policy—an appearance of conformity with the majority will—prescribed the Czar's public expressions and actions during the framing of the peace terms; but there can be no doubt that Alexander had been permanently impressed, as the other smoldering monarchs had not, by the emanation of godpower he had sensed and responded to from the time of his earliest conversations with the Emperor of the French. It was he who had first suggested Elba as a suitable place of withdrawal for the deposed dictator; likewise it was he who had proposed that the French treasury provide the new Elban king with the pension of two million francs annually with which to keep up his state. He could insist on this provision being written into the treaty—but that was as far as his influence could extend: Not a sou was ever paid, the honor of all the royal signatories notwithstanding. Poverty—the inability of Napoleon to support Elba any longer from the resources of his own pocket—was one of the chief reasons for his return.

Finally, the fact that Alexander sent to St. Helena as his representative a sensitive and cultured diplomat, a man of superior caliber—encouraging him to write down in his reports every detail and observation he could recall—attests to his continued fascination with the prodigious personality of the prisoner and the permanent impact of their momentous and stimulating friendship.

Napoleon was frequently to express his regret that he had not surrendered himself to the Russians rather than to the British, after Waterloo, since he realized that the affectionate regard once existing between himself and Alexander might have procured for him a more tolerable exile with a less rigorous style of restraint

WHO LIES HERE?

than the one devised for him in London. Several attempts were made by members of Napoleon's staff to induce Count Balmain to accept letters written by their master to the Czar, forwarding them in the immunity of his diplomatic pouches to Russia. Accounts of these efforts appear in Balmain's reports, always accompanied by the description of his firm refusal to cooperate in any such subterfuges. One need not be so certain that he did refuse, however. He may well have been advised, by his ministry, as to his appropriate conduct in such events—and it is most certain that the Russian Emperor would have been understandably intrigued by the contents of such messages, and not loath to receive them.

No one is quite sure why Balmain should have made such a point of refusing to accept these proffered letters, in any event: He had previously and without any hesitation accepted and forwarded Napoleon's *Observations on Lord Bathurst's Speech*—and this would have been, in Lowe's eyes, as dangerous a freedom as would the forwarding of any conceivable correspondence originating in Longwood. Accordingly, there is reason to disregard Balmain's too-emphatic accounts of his refusals to accept mail from the prisoner, and to consider them as a part of a structure designed to stress both his and his ministry's incorruptibility concerning clandestine activity on Napoleon's behalf.

What may have actually been the ultimate relationship between Balmain and the prisoner he was supposed to watch can only be speculated on, in the light of the above observations. It is certain that in November of 1818 Alexander reported harshly and unfavorably to the Congress of Aix when the question of better treatment for Napoleon was raised—appearing to insist on an increased rigor, rather than a relaxation, in the restrictions created by Hudson Lowe. But this message was sent well after the date when Gourgaud had "changed his mind" in London, being assured from his timetable that the Eagle had taken flight. This too is a

TOKENS AND TESTAMENTS

strange thing, that the Russian Emperor should at that particular time have apparently become converted to the doctrine of severity in Napoleon's imprisonment, when just prior to August his influence had been cast—as far as was expedient politically—in the direction of a more tolerable exile.

A typical comment of Balmain's on the nature of the sort of treatment the prisoner was receiving is this report to the Czar: "Nothing could be more absurd, more impolitic and less generous than this treatment of Napoleon by the English." Alexander, it is well known, rightly prized the opinions of his representative on St. Helena. In view of this, the monarch's recommendation of "greater severity" to the Congress of Aix might well appear to have been dictated by the desire to free himself of any suspicion, in the eyes of historians of that time or of the future, of having in any way connived through his minister's acts in the disappearance of Bonaparte from his island.

At any rate, Count Balmain left Jamestown for Rio de Janeiro on August 22, 1818—announcedly for his health, shattered by the arduous nature of his duties in shadowing the prisoner, no doubt. Before embarking on the *David,* he made a strange and perhaps significant comment to Major Gorrequer, Lowe's aide and secretary: a remark the major thought worthy of inclusion in his recently released diaries. Alone and solitary Balmain's observation stands, with no comment. He said, *"Il n'y a plus d'interressant."* ["Nothing more of any interest here!"]

This Major Gorrequer plays but a minor role in the St. Helena history, but his personality comes through the earlier scant references quite attractively. He was of Huguenot extraction, small, fair, alert and self-contained; at Plantation House he lived a constantly vexed life: Being a bachelor, he was assigned the worst quarters available and his rank, modest in comparison with that of the other aides, kept him to such tasks as copying Lowe's eternal

WHO LIES HERE?

correspondence and rewriting his orders as fast as the Governor's mind should be changed. His diary was obviously kept as a means of blowing off steam accumulated in the repressions of each arduous day, and only recently was it released by the British government and published.

That it had been kept under wraps for so long, coupled with the fact that the writer had had a known sympathy for the French exiles and a supreme contempt for the officialdom at Plantation House, had led a good many writers to speculate ardently on the possible presence of excitingly revealing material in the major's notes. The reason given for the long delay in permitting access to them is that a longstanding lawsuit might thereby have been undesirably influenced. It is impossible to see how these rather petty revelations could have caused harm to anyone or anything, today or a century ago—they deal with gossip about Lady Lowe's proclivities, anecdotes of Lowe's imbecilities, family arguments and the like. That remark of Balmain's just before his boat sailed—that there was nothing more of interest there—comes as close to the nature of a dangerous implication as exists in the entire book.

One can only muse on the meaning of this strange sentence—and wonder too why it was made just then, and why Major Gorrequer, that secretive, thoughtful, observing type of man, should have considered such a casual sort of offering worthy of the labor of recording—out of all else Balmain might have had to say at that juncture.

Why, what had happened, that there would be nothing, or rather that there was nothing, of any further interest?

Not too much illumination is cast by a study of the young officer himself. Harried and bedeviled by Sir Hudson and constantly humiliated by his lady, daily subjected to Sir Thomas Reade's boorish and clumsy breaches of decorum or seemly conduct—he yet managed to maintain an appearance of tight-lipped indiffer-

TOKENS AND TESTAMENTS

ence to these exasperations, nightly relieving his overcharged soul into the pages of his journal, furtively kept and concealed. It is recorded of him that for the remainder of his life, whenever the subject of Napoleon's detention on St. Helena was brought up, he maintained a strict silence and forever refused to speak of his experiences there. Under these circumstances it is not too likely that the major would have dared to confide any secret knowledge he might have come by to the pages of his journal, even in his system of partial code. And yet those little confidences about Lady Lowe's affinity for the gin bottle would, had they been come upon by one of Reade's spying agents, have sent the writer in disgrace back to England as swiftly as would some more momentous reference. One can only speculate as to whether this diary, so long buried in a musty vault, has been released in its entirety.

At all events it is well demonstrated that Gorrequer was a man who knew how to keep his own counsel. If he did indeed know or suspect anything of the strange movements between Longwood and Jamestown harbor, he doubtless did well to keep such things to himself—such knowledge could well have occasioned the ruin or even the death of the man rash enough to commit it to writing.

After a four-month holiday spent in Rio, during which one may presume the overwrought commissioner of the Czar relieved himself of the several pressures built up by the Spartan conditions of his existence on the island, Count Balmain returned to St. Helena "a changed man," to employ Reade's phrase in his report to the governor. This was but natural: All this time he had been freed from the exasperations of dealing with the erratic notions of the lord of Plantation House; he had reveled in the novel sights and sounds of a strange city, as well as occupying himself, perhaps, in some barely conceivable travel arrangements and procurement of ships' passages. "The Count was a changed man," Reade went on,

WHO LIES HERE?

"and he has quite altered his opinion in regard to the French people at Longwood. He now thinks of them as 'a curious set'." This would seem yet another strange thing, since right up to the time of his departure for Rio, Balmain had at all times expressed a cultured tolerance for any seeming eccentricities in the behavior of the French and had many times attempted to interpret their reported deeds and conversation in a more lenient or tolerant manner than that in which the purple-faced Reade or the spluttering Lowe were inclined to consider them.

They are curious matters, these two reported statements as to something having changed, of things having lost their savor —made by the only man on the island possessing any real cultivation or sensibility. If there were nothing anymore of interest on St. Helena, one must ask why—for everything was, ostensibly, as it had been for almost three years: There were the same dissensions and bickerings between Longwood and the governor's mansion, between the Montholons and the Bertrands, between Sir Hudson and Lady Lowe, between Lady Lowe and those who maliciously conspired to conceal her gin supply so that she must attempt to survive on the sherry.

Balmain's remark is really devoid of any meaning that could ordinarily be assigned to it—and yet Major Gorrequer thought it of some significance, for it is the only word of Balmain's that he recorded for this occasion. Sequentially, when the commissioner had returned to St. Helena after his four-month vacation, Reade was able to report that he had lost his former sympathetic regard for the Longwood people and now referred to them rather contemptuously as "a curious set." This expression was naturally taken to include the Emperor as well as the others of the little court— or so Lowe and Reade were meant to believe. Why should Napoleon, the Czar's friend and the subject of the Count's many urbane and commendatory observations to his government, have

TOKENS AND TESTAMENTS

so suddenly become an object of slightly supercilious indifference?

One conceivable answer would be that Balmain knew that the heart and spirit of Longwood had departed and that from then on a rather dreary masquerade would be all that remained for him to observe. He would continue to do all that remained in his power to preserve the illusion from any blundering interference—the Czar would expect as much from him as long as he was retained on the island. But from then on the less attention directed to Longwood the better. An attitude on his part of mild boredom and indifference would create the best possible protection he could afford the household and its secret, as least likely to arouse Hudson Lowe's lurking fears and suspicions.

It is of course quite impossible to say how the transfer of the two men was carried out. If the secret was ever put on paper—and a mad act that would have been!—it was either burned in the holocaust of documents carried out by Bertrand and Montholon before their departure in 1821 or was buried with the other secret material in the grounds about Longwood. For reasons of state, as well as for family considerations, a revelation of this nature could never be made public—even after the intervening century and a half.

Nevertheless we can at least venture on a reproduction of the possible method, attempting as far as we may to duplicate the thought processes of those who contrived it.

It has been shown how Napoleon had, in the earlier period, refused to avail himself of several proffered plans of escape. Quite aside from the outstanding objection that any of these would have wrecked his paramount purpose of creating that myth of martyrdom for his legend, he had also a strong aversion to the impairment of his dignity by recourse to such entirely practicable means as were suggested to him—the concealment of his person in one of

WHO LIES HERE?

the empty food barrels to be returned to Jamestown or the adoption of a Chinese disguise in order to accompany a group of these toilers in their unsupervised movements about the island. Were he to have been discovered thus a roar of mocking laughter would have traveled around the world—a thing worse in his imagination than even this solitary death itself. The scaling of the rock walls of the island would into the bargain have been impossible for anyone not a mountaineer—which consideration eliminated yet other suggested methods of evasion.

The preferable way—the only way consonant with his conception of his fame and prestige—would be to issue casually forth from Longwood, in broad daylight, in the full view of any and all concerned. There was only one practicable route down from the domicile of the French to the docks of Jamestown—the main roadway passing first the Devil's Punchbowl, Hutt's Gate and the Alarm House; then came the increasingly steep slope down past The Briars, Balcombe's old home, where he had first lodged and met young Betsy. Two and a half miles of this steep descent, then through Jamestown by its main street and down to the stone quay and beyond: The ultimate solid shelter of the *David* swinging at her anchor in the open harbor. The two men who had come ashore that morning—one of them stocky, short, heavily bearded—had obtained, at the charge of the ship, a light wagon and a team of horses, transferring to it several wooden crates they had brought ashore in the ship's boat. These crates were invoiced as fancy foods and wines, all of them addressed to General Bonaparte at Longwood House. They were marked as sent by Lord and Lady Holland, London, and when Sir Thomas Reade had gone on board the previous afternoon to inspect these and other shipments for St. Helena, he had passed them after only the most cursory survey coupled with some of his usual slighting comments. There had been several such shipments from Lord Holland in the past

TOKENS AND TESTAMENTS

months—and Plantation House had become cautious about creating unpleasant incidents in that quarter. This liberal peer and his lady were leaders in England in the movement of sympathy and compassion for the French, and in practical means of expressing their sentiments.

Two of the crew to go ashore, a cart to be found. Very well—for how long? For as long as it took to drive to the General's house and back, with perhaps a bit over to wet their whistles in the kitchen? Permission granted.

It was the clean-shaven one who drove the wagon and who got them checked past the sentry at Hutt's Gate, showing Sir Thomas' permit. His companion, he indicated, was a foreigner and spoke no English. When the two returned, an hour or so later, the same sentry passed them on, the bearded stocky man hunched in the seat and staring stupidly straight ahead. They tied the team where they had found it, then clambered down into the boat, the bearded one sitting impassive in the stern as his comrade pulled for the *David*. Reade, watching from his office window at the Castle, noted the time and checked it on the ship's chargebill.

Count Balmain, too, preparing his papers for boarding, may have been there with him—unobtrusively studying the two crewmen until they went up the ship's side and vanished behind her bulwarks—slowly, and with commendable deliberation.

As the two had passed along the quay below him, he had wondered a little about the beard. Had Robeaud brought an artificial one with him—or even worn it himself rather than grow his own—or could the Emperor have grown one himself in the last few weeks, while remaining indoors? Well—he would learn the answers to all these things tomorrow; the crossing to Rio promised to be an interesting one indeed, but it was going to seem a long wait until the *David* was permitted to clear the harbor.

* * *

WHO LIES HERE?

And from Rio? Once arrived there and of course all the world was available. There was also the famous center of loyal and active Bonapartists and old soldiers; even Pauline Fourès herself was reputed to have made her home in the midst of the colony. But had Napoleon thought it permissible to let himself be heard of by even one of that devoted group, the wide world would inevitably have learned of it—and no such tradition exists. He could have gone on to America and joined his brother Joseph on his magnificent estate at Bordentown, New Jersey; no doubt he weighed the decision carefully, this appealing vision, before rejecting it. Too much prominence—and after all, he had a paramount duty to his "alter ego" and the friends on St. Helena: The identity of the prisoner must never be put in question, nor the safety of the household into jeopardy. If the British ever learned of the great deception practiced on them, they would get at him by employing the utmost severity against Robeaud and the other conspirators—death or long terms of the harshest imprisonment would be the lot of all involved.

Even beyond all that was the supremely important legend-building scheme in which Longwood was engaged: Robeaud was destined to die there in the near future, as he had confessed to Napoleon in the brief hour the two men had shared as they changed clothes with each other. The doctor in Verdun had given him three years of life at the utmost, provided there was a regime of proper diet, rest and care. This, although unfortunate for the man himself, was nevertheless all to the good regarding the prospects of the Emperor. He had but to maintain himself in some obscure activity, to lie low, until the news arrived of the passing of Longwood's tenant—to the world, the end of the great Napoleon.

According to the legend he went to live in Verona. The choice of a diamond merchant as a business partner would have had considerable appeal: The Bonapartes all believed in diamonds as the best

TOKENS AND TESTAMENTS

form of portable wealth. By the time he had communicated with the most trustworthy members of his family there would be no lack of baubles such as these—but suspicion might have attached itself to a private individual who disposed of large numbers of jewels of the richest variety, whereas as a merchant he could find a market for them without drawing undue attention to himself. There was, moreover, the considerable savings in commissions to be kept in mind!

Verona might well have appealed to him with stirring memories of his earliest campaigns in northern Italy—when, as he had admitted at Longwood, he had been more truly happy than ever again in his career. "I was only twenty-six," he had told his companions, "but I foresaw then what I might become. It was as though I were being lifted high into the air and the world disappearing beneath my feet!" Enough reason, such a memory, to bring a man back to so beautiful a country, where he might dwell hidden, savoring life calmly, until perhaps the time should come when he would recover his old enthusiasm for involvement and the undertaking of bold enterprises. But not until that news . . . three years he had said. . . .

A strange feeling, this being dead and yet living! Often he heard people discussing him, speaking of his great deeds; of his crimes too, some denouncing him, but most approving. He read many of the books written about him and his wars and wished that those of Las Cases and O'Meara and Gourgaud were published, so that he might see how they were shaping his impressive story. It is more than probable that he confided in his mother, perhaps too in Joseph and in Pauline. But not, of course, in his Empress Marie Louise, she who was living in open contempt of morality with her Count Neipperg, bearing him illegitimate children.

And his son, the King of Rome?

No doubt the father early discovered that his real reason for

WHO LIES HERE?

selecting a city in northern Italy to be his home was because of its comparative proximity—with safety—to Vienna, the seat of his implacable foe, the Austrian Emperor, the man whom he had once compelled to offer his daughter in marriage, and who had never forgiven him for this humiliation! Vienna, and Castle Schönbrunn, where he had twice lived as a conqueror—now the virtual prison of his son. His loved son, now known as the Duke of Reichstadt: He had once declared that he would prefer to see that son dead than have him brought up as an Austrian prince. He was not even a prince, but only a duke, a prisoner brought up in ignorance of his father's glorious career—and France was far and feeble now, and hope for a better future seemed futile. Still, one never knew what turns of Fortune's wheel were in store: It was always well to be ready and prepared for the jade's smile, like a skilled gambler. God knew he had experienced more of those smiles than most men, before all went sour! So, were he ever to be needed or if a resolute deed were required to rescue his beloved boy, there he would be: not a long journey off, safe there from the threat of Austrian spies and Metternich's devilish network. He had crossed those Alps before—he knew the road!

From time to time he wondered how Robeaud was faring. He must write again, the years were beginning to slip by—it was high time to let them have the notes for his will, which Robeaud would copy out in extended form. He congratulated himself on not having required to touch his own fortune nor those funds at Lafitte's—an impossibility anyway, without an exposure of his true identity. Now he would proceed to dispose of it all in proper fashion; Robeaud's handwriting, as noted in several letters received from the island in the first months, was uncannily like his own—but still far too legible. That, however, would be put down to the writer's advanced illness and weakness, to his urgent desire to make his last testament clear and indisputable. Montholon

TOKENS AND TESTAMENTS

could write some comment to that effect; he and Bertrand would sign it as well, and their witness would certainly suffice.

On the morning of April 13, 1821, Robeaud was seized by griping pains and a severe bout of vomiting. The ulcer at his pyloric valve was active again: It would bring about his death in three weeks. The writing of the will had been deferred too long in the hope that each day might find the victim strong enough to tackle the long transcription. That same afternoon, by a great effort of will, he compelled himself to begin.

First, however, Count Montholon took the unusual precaution of bolting the bedroom door; he then unlocked the desk and removed the sheaf of notes, all written in a minute script on both sides of flimsy paper. For three hours Montholon deciphered these, Robeaud occasionally aiding him in the elucidation of the outrageous scrawl, the Count reading in a low voice and the dying man writing in his acquired orthography—yet forcing himself to leave the sentences legible.

The account of the writing of the will is supplied by Count Montholon alone and there was at no time any other witness; as he states, at each session the door was bolted and no others were admitted—with mention of an exception that illustrates the ritual. Dr. Arnott had arrived to check with Antommarchi on the condition of his patient; before the door was unbolted and Arnott admitted, the entire mass of papers was first put into the inner cabinet of the desk, then both drawer and desk were locked securely. These same procedures were again gone through on the fifteenth of the month, when ten or twelve more pages were written out with "a trembling hand," as Montholon testifies.

But it seems that in distant Verona Napoleon was having yet more afterthought. A new package of instructions had arrived and on the twenty-fifth the unfortunate Robeaud, in spite of being "shaken by convulsions, mouth bitter with his nausea," wrote out a series of codicils to the will. Fortunately, although there was a lot of additional material—specific and complex instructions for the three executors, advice about the upbringing of his son, letters to be sent to his bankers and the treasurers of his estates—all this Montholon could write himself as though from Napoleon's dictation. All that was required of the invalid was his scrawled signature or initial. In addition he addressed all the envelopes himself.

Everything was attended to, it appeared. The will and other documents would all be franked from St. Helena, all of them written on paper bearing the well-known British watermark dated 1819—the only kind of legal paper obtainable in Jamestown. The will, the codicils and the letters could defy any inspection, for any irregularity in the handwriting would be attributable to the patient's moribund condition, to his determination to force his handwriting into legibility. Beyond that there were the signatures of three trustworthy executors, as well as the verbal evidence of the two doctors.

Of Napoleon's handwriting Méneval had observed, in earlier days, "it was a hodge-podge of disconnected letters, quite illegible. Half of the letters were lacking in every word—he could not himself make out what he had written." To this day much of his scribbling has to be guessed at; only his employment of secretaries—even on the battlefield—enabled him to record his thoughts or wishes. And yet a commentator writes of the will that the writing is "neat and legible"!

In the ultimate analysis of the will's genuineness, however, posterity has asked only this question: Who but Napoleon himself could have carried that encyclopedic mental record of his scattered properties, of that long list of beneficiaries, many of them obscure people (there were ninety-seven) remembered from the days of his early struggles? Montholon would have been able, no doubt, to flesh out the bare bones of the smuggled script—both from notes left with him by Napoleon and from his intimate knowledge of the latter's wishes—so often expressed to him in turns of phrase and sentence identifiable as the imperial manner.

It should be kept in mind that the Count was, by his own testimony, the only man in the world who saw that last document written, his alone is the description of how it was done. The other two executors were excluded from the bedchamber, as previously mentioned—their seals and signatures were affixed afterward; it was not until they were all aboard the transport *Camel* and on their way to England that each learned of his legacy. Poor Bertrand found he was to receive much less than he had expected—only a quarter of Montholon's share and but little more than Marchand's.

Nevertheless the two were both able and willing, as already recounted, to make up a sum for Gourgaud out of their legacies —even though it turned out that Napoleon had greatly overestimated his wealth and that the individual bequests could only be paid in part. (Under the Second Empire a Treasury appropriation was made to enable all of the items to be paid in full, to the descendents if not to the principals themselves.) The fact that General Gourgaud's name was left out of the will seemed natural enough to everyone, for in official Bonapartist circles he was regarded as renegade and traitor, one who had done his helpless master enormous harm by his indiscretions and outright falsehoods. Strangely enough Parisian Napoleonists and the companions of St. Helena by no means appeared to share these opinions —and by 1840 it was obvious that neither did the Royalists, for it was they who included Gourgaud in the honorable company of the other survivors of Longwood sent to St. Helena to recover the body from that uninscribed tomb in Geranium Valley. On their return

WHO LIES HERE?

Gourgaud, riding in triumph toward Les Invalides beside that monumental hearse, was acclaimed by the throngs as vociferously as were Bertrand and Marchand.

In actuality the excesses of Gourgaud's revelations had caused little harm at Longwood—it had been foreseen by the conspirators that there would inevitably be an increase in severity of the supervision, some tightening of the restrictions. But these were immediately all to the good since they resulted in the pseudo-Emperor being the more closely confined within the limits of the house and grounds—as he wished to be, without doubt, and as the others preferred to have him until he became more habituated to his part. The fatal progress of Robeaud's disease had been made known to the staff, and it was well understood that nothing the British contrived could worsen his prospects nor accelerate his demise. This last, sadly enough, was for the entire Longwood household a consummation devoutly to be wished—*the quicker he goes the better,* as they might have crudely expressed it: On this one life the tantalizing prospect of immediate freedom for them all was contingent. This was not, well considered, so very brutal an attitude; only death could free this man from his extraordinary situation—and surely his passing, inevitable even had he remained undisturbed on the wretched farm in Baleicourt, would be rendered more endurable, more meaningful, under the circumstances provided for him on St. Helena?

So there were no genuine regrets at his end; nor was Gourgaud, then made free of his homeland once again, long obliged to forfeit any of his self-esteem or to be denied the happy approval of his returned compatriots. The story of the subterfuges and deceptions he had practiced on the British was commonly circulated, as may be discovered in memoirs of the period—and no doubt much relished by the citizenry, for a tide of revulsion was setting in

TOKENS AND TESTAMENTS

against the reactionary Bourbon, as well as against the Duke of Wellington whose military ascendency and Tory influence provided the stiffening for that monarch's policies. On the other hand, the Emperor's star was once again in ascendency. The legend had taken on form and substance, was filling out, and all it required to reach full stature was the publication of the several journals and diaries compiled by the assiduous Longwood veterans—these, plus a little political adversity for France to create a nostalgia for the vanished days of glory.

Of these volumes of reminiscenses, perhaps the one least veracious as to details is Montholon's. In strict obedience to Napoleon's request he was to defer publication of his *Récits de la captivité de Napoléon à Sainte Hélène* until twenty-five years after the "Emperor's" death. (Did Napoleon consider that that period might cover his own lifespan? At all events the book did not appear until 1847.) It has been found acceptable only when its account is supported by one or more of the others, for Montholon was inclined to give his imagination a loose rein, creating many an instance of preposterous or unlikely scenes.

Gourgaud's book, on the other hand, is accepted as being rigorously correct—even in those instances where the truth might seem to have done the writer small service. His text serves as a criterion of the other reports—of course only up to the time he left Longwood. His acknowledged veracity and careful detail are worth noting in the final assessment of the nature of his services in 1818, as well as in the evaluation of his essential character. Some of his original material has been edited out of the later edition of his *Journal de Sainte Hélène*, thus lending support to the belief that the original version had been doctored or contrived to impress Lowe with the Baron's truthfulness had the manuscript been confiscated. It was held back from the public until 1899; Count

WHO LIES HERE?

Bertrand's coded *Cahiers de Sainte Hélène* were only brought to light in midcentury, deciphered and published in 1959. There is yet more of the *Cahiers* unavailable in English translation.

It should be evident then that the writing of the will need have represented no difficulty that Robeaud and Montholon could not readily have surmounted; neither would the production of any other written document—orders, messages, instructions—which would have been to the household's common advantage to show to the British and the world at large—whether before the prisoner's death, or afterward. Without doubt innumerable notes and memoranda in Napoleon's own hand had been left, and these could, if required, be postdated and represented as products of any given period between 1819 and 1821. Other orders could be composed in that interval and written as though received from Napoleon's dictation, with the scrawled initial applied. Accounts of conversations with the Emperor could be put together in his characteristically pungent or incisive phraseology from some part of the mountainous mass of notes accumulated in the first years, or from retained recollections of hours of private conversations.

There is, in brief, no account purporting to constitute a record of Napoleon's acts or words or the revelations of his unique mind, after 1818, which could not have been contrived with the greatest ease by the deliberate collaboration of Bertrand, Montholon and Marchand—in one or another of the three ways mentioned: by a selection from the copious writings left with them, by collusion from their joint memories, or by the creation through Robeaud of yet others as seemed desirable. The descriptions of the last hours of the doomed man were, of course, derived from direct observation of Robeaud, since the severity of his ultimate symptoms was (fortunately for all concerned except the wretched victim) but an exacerbation of those general disturbances of which Napoleon had often complained.

TOKENS AND TESTAMENTS

Curiously there is but one place where the different accounts show no sign of general agreement, and that is in the matter of the dying man's last words. It seems that here each writer wished to put in something significant, some suggestion of the magnificent heights to which the presumed Emperor, in his terminal delirium, had access. These words had always a suspicious "staginess" about them—"Josephine," "the Head of the Army" and others, as well as some intolerable nonsense by Montholon. It took the arrival of Bertrand's book to suggest that there were none of these at all —and his report is not suspect; he stood as near the mouth of the dying as any other, and he was an unexcitable rational sort of man. The references to Josephine and to military activity were no doubt devised by the writers to give one last touch of authenticity: what the world would expect at the deathbed of the great Napoleon. But for some reason unknown they were not made to correspond; perhaps the accounts were written down much later, and when the authors were separated or unable to confer.

Death had come for Robeaud at the end of the day—there were none of the violent convulsions of nature that superstitious awe was later to evolve: no storm, no trees torn out by the roots. The island records tell of a calm and peaceful evening as a conclusion was written to the poor man's sufferings. All the Longwood "family" were present, including Madame Bertrand and a British physician; Lowe had been instantly informed, but it was not until the next day that he was invited to enter the dead prisoner's home and to look on his body—as he had last done, he believed, on the day of their ultimate rupture in 1816. Now that prisoner lay before him on his couch, fully uniformed as of old—the famous cocked hat in place, his torso draped in the purple cloak of Marengo, his countenance prepared with assiduous care by the valets, astounding

WHO LIES HERE?

everyone who has left a record of his emotions by its unbelievable youth and serenity.

Lowe turned to the Marquis de Montchenu, who accompanied him, and asked, "Do you recognize him?" To which the French commissioner replied, "I do."

Now it is difficult to guess how many years may have elapsed since Montchenu had seen Napoleon in Europe—for it is very certain that he had never looked on him in St. Helena. Indeed, it is more than probable that he had never in his life beheld the Emperor, since he had fled France at the time of the revolution and become an *émigré*, returning to Paris with the final restoration of the Bourbons. A supreme and ultimate example, this, of the delusive nature of all that "overwhelmingly convincing evidence, the daily and even hourly observations" of Bonaparte's presence and activities on the island! The governor, incredibly, had not set eyes on his prisoner in five years—and the Frenchman in all probability had never done so, certainly not on St. Helena—and these were the two who officially "identified" the dead man, for the historical and political record!

Lowe gave his permission for an autopsy to be conducted, and on the day afterward the islanders and the men and officers of the garrison and the fleet would be permitted to file by and pay their last respects to one who—as these people were slowly beginning to comprehend—was forever to be included among the world's most great.

Over and over we are told by the different witnesses, in very much the same terms, that the face of the dead was that of a man in his early thirties—"that of the Napoleon of the Consulate"—"a face of incredible beauty." Dr. Shortt, the chief medical officer of the island, wrote that "his face was in death the most beautiful that I have ever beheld, exhibiting softness and every good expression in the highest degree." These phrases were being employed to describe—presumably—a man of fifty-two years of age; a broken emperor, long bowed in despair and the bitter knowledge of his own miscalculations, racked for months by the intolerable pains of his lingering death.

If his body was, for the first time since 1818, now allowed to be viewed at close range by any who chose to do so, then why not before?

Perhaps, as suggested previously, because the eyes now permanently closed were of another color than the blue-gray widely known as that of the Emperor's own, and so depicted in many well-known portraits. Perhaps because the teeth, sealed now behind the closed lips, were bad or deficient, whereas Napoleon's were famed for their regularity and whiteness. The hair, in some matter of color or growth, might have caused attention had not the hat been in place. Who can say, exactly, what details were discrepant—but have there ever been two men born on this earth, identical twins excepted, who were absolute reproductions of each other in every respect and category? The poise of the head, the manner of regard, the tone, pitch or timbre of the voice—a score of such individualities will rise to distinguish them, even though for a few silent and deliberately posed moments they may appear to be startlingly alike.

At two P.M. on May 6 the body of the deceased was laid along a plank trestle table set up in what was once designated "the billiard room," while a group of seventeen men was admitted. These were of the two parties, English and French. Eight of them were doctors, or what were by courtesy or custom so styled. Seven of these medical men were British, the other being the Corsican Antommarchi, that highly qualified dissector. Since he had also

WHO LIES HERE?

been the official Longwood "physician," he was as a courtesy permitted to conduct the autopsy while the others either assisted when needed, or merely watched.

The chief of the British group was Thomas Shortt, who therefore wrote the report of the autopsy and was the first to append his name to it—he adds, after his degree, "Chief Medical Officer and Physician." The distinction between a physician and a surgeon has come to be much less stressed than formerly, when the surgeon —at least in the armed services—tended to be a man of less training and background, a more rough-and-ready type who had often acquired his ruthless skills (this was in the days prior to the discovery of anesthetics) "on the job," so to speak.

The fourth signature to this document is that of "Francis Burton, M.D., Surgeon 66th Reg't." This name is of some interest also, for two months previously the doctor had become uncle of a child destined to achieve fame in years to come as Sir Richard Burton—explorer, Orientalist and celebrated translator of the *Arabian Nights*. It was this same Dr. Burton who was enterprising enough, and sufficiently ingenious, to go out in a small boat and at risk of his life gather some raw gypsum from which to manufacture plaster of paris, therewith to take an impression of the dead man's features. From this quite good impression derive the various "death masks" existing today in the museums of Europe.

Because Antommarchi was nominally Napoleon's personal physician, he resented the fact that he was not to write the official report of the autopsy—a viewpoint further justified by the general agreement that he should be the one permitted to wield the scalpel; accordingly he later on declined to put his name to Shortt's report, but instead wrote one of his own for the instruction of Lowe and the world in general. His is the most complete, and of far greater significance and interest than the official report. Doctors Henry and Rutledge, classified as assistant surgeons, were not

TOKENS AND TESTAMENTS

asked to sign; later on, however, each was to write his own partial version and to include details of much interest which appear neither in the official version nor in Antommarchi's amplified one.

It at once becomes evident that Antommarchi, with some others of the French group, no longer felt himself under the arbitrary thumb of Sir Hudson Lowe: Besides declining to give his endorsement to the report, he included in his own version a bold observation on the abnormal appearance of the liver—a matter that Shortt, in deference to the governor's expressed wish, had played down. It had early become apparent that Lowe would not countenance the recording of such a condition since it would carry the implication that Napoleon had been exposed to hepatitis (as O'Meara and Stokoe had charged) while under British supervision. This disease was certainly endemic on the island in those days, as the deaths of a great many British soldiers and sailors attest, and neither the home government nor its servant Lowe wished to provide the Liberals and Bonapartists of that time nor of the future, with means of asserting that deliberate indifference or even active malice on the part of his captors had contributed to the shortening of the Emperor's life.

The presence of a perforated gastric ulcer near the pyloric orifice was, naturally and quite obviously, the immediate cause of death—even if not of the increasing debility and malaise of the patient during the last two or three years of his life. To do Thomas Shortt credit, he had in his first draft included the statement (but only under Antommarchi's prodding) that "the liver was a little larger than normal"; Lowe had promptly insisted on a new report with this phrase removed. Such was the fear inspired by this tyrant that a new report was made—Shortt was not unaware that the governor had already broken and ruined two other doctors who had failed to defer to his will on this matter of hepatitis—and was signed again by the British medical men (including a Dr. Livingstone who had not been present through more than a minor part of the autopsy). The first report, bearing a comment in its margin by Shortt stating that the "liver" clause was to be removed by order of Sir Hudson Lowe, exists today in private ownership.

Antommarchi, recklessly defiant, wrote that "the spleen and liver, which was hardened, were very large and distended." This version was published in 1825 in the doctor's book and attracted a great deal of attention, for although the man was poorly regarded as a physician, he was throughout his career recognized as an anatomist of the best training and experience. On the basis of his testimony, as well as on that of Shortt's suppressed version, one may well conclude that hepatitis contracted on the island contributed in no small degree to the rapid decline, after 1819, of the prisoner.

Here it may be suggested that the diagnosis of cancer of the stomach agreed on by all present, and still popularly cherished, ought once and for all to be discarded. No physician of today would diagnose a tumorous or inflamed area as malignant without a thorough histopathological examination; of course this technique and knowledge was still unknown in their current medical practice. As carefully described by Antommarchi there was no evidence of metastasis (the spreading or extension of the morbid area), nor of any involvement of the adjacent lymph nodes. There was no cachexia, or wasting away of the body tissues—rather the opposite. From these observations plus the description of the ulcerous area itself, most of today's diagnosticians who have reviewed the facts of the case are in agreement that the penetration of the stomach wall was *per se* quite sufficient to produce the agonies and eventual death of the afflicted man—with an assist, beyond doubt, from the infected liver.

The first part of Antommarchi's report deals, quite properly, with the general appearance and dimensions of the body. The

TOKENS AND TESTAMENTS

official report has none of this invaluable material, so that it is only here that one may learn of the various scars of old wounds that the dissector noticed in his examination, or learn of the painstaking measurements he took in accord with the Continental custom.

His report tells us that "there were several scars, namely, one on the head, three on the left leg—one of which was on the *malleolus externus* (the outer ankle bone); one was at the extremity of the *digitis annularis* (the ring finger) of the left hand, and several in the left thigh."

In his entire career Napoleon received but two wounds. The first was at the siege of Toulon in 1793, where he led an infantry attack; his horse was killed under him and he was struck by the pike of a British Marine sergeant. The wound was on the inner side of the left thigh, just above the knee. According to Las Cases it had left a very deep scar, for at the time the wound became infected and the surgeon had wished to amputate. It seems strange that Antommarchi would dismiss this scar as apparently being one of the "several in the left thigh." Las Cases appears to have been awed by the size of it. The second wound was received at the siege of Regensberg in 1809, where a musket ball struck the right heel causing *"forte contusion du droit pied."*

Not only does the scrupulous Antommarchi make no mention at all of scars on the right leg or body, but he records a number of which there is no other history: several in the left thigh, more on the lower left leg, on the finger, the head. It is as impossible to dispute these findings as those of the Army Medical Service, and yet the two are considerably at variance. One might reflect that the infantryman Robeaud had been a combat soldier before he was plucked from the ranks to serve the Emperor in person—and that wounds on the left side of the body rather than the right would be those most likely to be incurred in hand-to-hand fighting with the bayonet, since the left side is that chiefly to the fore.

WHO LIES HERE?

At any event it is an unarguable fact that the records—first of Napoleon's actual wounds, second of the scars borne by his presumed cadaver—do not correspond. The wound scars recorded by Antommarchi would appear to be those of another individual than Napoleon.

Now to the consideration of an intriguing observation that neither Dr. Shortt nor Antommarchi saw fit to include in their respective reports. It was given to Hudson Lowe by Dr. Henry, the assistant surgeon of the twentieth regiment, no doubt because of the peculiar interest the phenomenon held for him. Expressing himself most chastely in Latin, the doctor wrote, in a description of the genital area of the deceased: *partes viriles exiguitates, insignis sicut pueri,* or that the sexual organs were small, like those of a boy. There was little or no pubic hair, nor any hair on the body. Summing up, Dr. Henry added "the whole genital system of the deceased seemed to show a physical basis for the absence of sexual desire and for the continence which are known to have been characteristic of him."

One must presume that Dr. Henry was referring only to the prisoner's latter years on the island when he spoke of this characteristic continence, for such a phrase could hardly have been employed to describe the sex life of the Emperor prior to his downfall—or even during his first years on St. Helena, if gossip may be believed. Possibly too much has been made of Napoleon's amorous proclivities by authors eager to turn out sensational volumes, for it is certain that almost any of his contemporaries —princes of the royal houses of Europe or England—ran up Venusian scores that by comparison would have made his look like those of an anchorite—here, indeed, was the traditional sport of kings. Nevertheless, his various *affaires* are recorded, as well as the brisk and businesslike manner he practiced in attaining to any particular prize that had caught his observant eye. Such seasoned women of the world as Grassini, the singer, famous figures of the stage, such as Mesdemoiselles George and Mars, with other ravishing actresses of the period—all were in their turn recipients of imperial favor; nor did the more attractive ladies of Josephine's entourage, titled women and many others of international renown, escape his assault—right up to the end of the reign. As in battle his attack was always impetuous, his appetite (when state affairs were not too demanding) seemingly insatiable.

Now it would appear more than likely that had the Emperor been no better furnished for what he sometimes humorously referred to as "the little business" than Dr. Henry's report implies, two or three at the least of these amiable ladies would, sooner or later, have let fall some indiscreet and unkind reference to so unlikely a shortcoming in so virile-reputed a man: out of pique, perhaps, or from thwarted ambition, or merely to satisfy that common desire to show a convincing proof of one's intimacy with the great. But it is not recorded that any one of these good ladies was, either at the time or in later years, so uncharitable or vindictive. What uproarious delight such a revelation would have provided those brutally ribald cartoonists across the Channel —Cruikshank, Gillray, *et al*, ever on the alert for such wondrous new grist for their defamatory mills! One has only to consider what they did to their own Lord Nelson and his Emma to get a faint notion of the ridicule they would have heaped on their enemy, the Emperor Napoleon.

There were no such productions. On the contrary, reports of the Emperor's sexual athleticism multiplied until it became a matter proverbial, widely believed even to this day.

Here again one is puzzled to reconcile two images: on one hand, the amorous tiger, ever ready for a new prey, impassioned and remorseless in his ranging; on the other, a man who—quite apart from his terminal illness—had been obviously unfitted for any such pursuits, being, as Dr. Henry noted, only a boy sexually. Hardly the man to have drawn Madame Denuelle all the way to Malmaison on that dreary day when he left everything to give himself up to his enemies: she, who had not a thing to gain from him any more. She came to say farewell to the man she loved, as did Walewska also, each to show him the son he had given her; all of them were drowned in grief, although the son he loved best of all, the little King of Rome, had been spirited away to Austria and was lost to him. Three sons, women who never forgot but who remained loyal and loving even when all was long over—like poor Belilote in distant Rio!

As for the virility Napoleon displayed in the first three years of his captivity—there wasn't, of course, much scope for such things, and he well realized that he was being watched closely for any signs of loose behavior, which would have made juicy morsels for the British newspapers—and gone far to smirch his image in the popular mind. That the government was anxious to learn any scandalous details of Napoleon's private life which they might be able to turn to account is repellently observable from the account of a Dr. Baxter, for three years chief medical officer of St. Helena, who returned to England in 1819. Immediately on his arrival he received a note from Lord Bathurst to attend him at the Colonial Office.

"His first question was how Bonaparte was . . . did he go out or take any exercise. He was anxious to know whether Bonaparte had access to women, and whether it was thought that Mesdames Montholon and Bertrand were condescending. . . ."

Repellent is the *mot juste*.

Actually there were only these two ladies in any sense eligible; Madame Bertrand is reputed (by her husband!) to have held out to the last, but both this lady and General Gourgaud agreed that *la Montholon* had shared the Emperor's bed, and that her child Napoléone, born in 1817, resembled Napoleon more than either of the Montholons. This little girl lived to see the year 1907.

But if Dr. Henry's description could not conceivably have applied to the Emperor Napoleon, one can readily imagine it as being more applicable to a man of Robeaud's history and evident temperament. This man had remained unmarried and childless, living between the wars with his sister. At the last he had become extremely stout, so that he might very probably have been as eunuchoid as the postmortem observation suggests—a reflection of a chronic glandular dysfunction. His sudden corpulency in 1819 was noted by the British, whereas up to 1818 the report of Napoleon's visitors had been unanimously that he was firm, healthy, and by no means fat—as has been shown.

Napoleon, in the year given as that of his death, would have been almost fifty-two; Robeaud is stated to have been born on July 19, 1781, and was therefore dead at age forty. One is struck by the unanimity of the exclamations by the British observers as they looked for the first time on the features of a man whom they had every reason to believe would look all of his fifty-two years —and even more. Major Gorrequer attests, "I had never seen a face more handsome . . . a well-proportioned countenance such as he might have had some twelve or fourteen years ago. A dozen of those who saw him concurred in saying that he did not look at the utmost more than forty—and he certainly did not; even less, I think."

Again, "There lay the Napoleon of the Consulate, a young man of thirty, handsomer in death than ever in life."

Dr. Henry wrote: "Everyone exclaimed, 'How beautiful!' " To sum up, the testimony is overwhelming as to the unexpected

WHO LIES HERE?

beauty and youth of the deceased; the reference to his appearance being that of a man of no more than forty are curiously frequent, and Major Gorrequer appears to have spoken for the opinion of everyone. Curious, too, is the repetitious use of that adjective "beautiful," so unusual in the case of a man of martial mold.

Antommarchi commenced his physical description by recording several dimensions of the body, including the total height "from the top of the head to the heels," which he gives as five feet two inches "and four lines." This must be set against the height recorded at the military academy in 1785 as five feet five and one-half inches, when Napoleon had just turned sixteen years of age—as well as against the estimated heights noted by several observers as being about five feet seven inches—these occurring between the years 1815 to 1818.

We are obliged to conclude then, from all this postmortem evidence, that a reduction had taken place during the later years of the captivity amounting to some four or five inches in the Emperor's height and of twelve to twenty years in his apparent age; that his recorded wound scars were not in evidence—or perhaps one may have been (here one can only guess)—and that yet others were present where not accounted for in Baron Larrey's records; and finally that the well-attested amorous proclivities and accomplishments of Napoleon had all been a contrived myth, since it was clearly apparent that such performances—or even the desire for them—had been out of the question for this poor man so callously exposed on the crude plank table: the man the British still thought of as "General Bonaparte."

A most informative autopsy.

It seems proper to include here an extraordinary story which —although it may not be integral to the Robeaud account *per se*—is nevertheless of such pertinency, and vouched for by such eminent sponsors, that a writer would be worthy of blame who passed it by. It is to be discovered in the book *Madame Mère,* by Baron Larrey, son of the great surgeon of Napoleon's armies, and was narrated by Baron Colonna, master of the household of Napoleon's mother. Since no English translation appears to be available, I offer my own:

> The Chevalier Colonna, chamberlain to Her Highness, told Madame de Sartrouville, her secretary, who has put it in her book, of a most strange visit received by Madame Mère in person on the exact date of May 5, 1821. (Here follows a sheet of the journal *Le Capitole,* December 14, 1839):
> "A well-dressed stranger appeared in the afternoon of that day at the palace, desiring to be admitted to her presence. The doorman asked him if he had an appointment, without which Her Highness would receive no one. The stranger replied quietly that he had not applied for an audience but that he had the absolute duty of seeing Madame, to give her a message of the highest importance. The concierge refused to let him pass, but influenced by an authoritative insistence that compelled obedience, he finally led him into the antechamber. Here he found the servants and told one of them to bring the *valet de chambre*—that an unknown gentleman requested the honor of an interview with Her Highness on a most important matter.
> "The valet came and asked the man his name, so that he might announce him. He was answered impatiently to the effect that he would speak with no one except Madame in person. The valet so informed Madame, who was seated with her chamberlain and her compan-

WHO LIES HERE?

ion; she decided to receive the stranger, who was pacing in the antechamber in a sort of subdued agitation. Monsieur Colonna, the chamberlain, invited him to enter. The stranger, after thanking the chamberlain, went on into the salon and greeted Madame with respect, while making it clear that he wished to have the honor of speaking to her without witnesses. Thereupon M. Colonna and Mlle. Mellini, at a signal from Madame, withdrew to an adjacent room—from which they could return at the faintest call for help.

"The unknown man came close to Madame and spoke to her of the Emperor, as though he had just left him. 'At this moment I am speaking,' he said to Her Highness, 'Napoleon is delivered from his pain and trouble: He is happy!' Then, while saying this, he put his hand into his breast (Her Highness believing that he was about to draw a dagger); instead he took out a crucifix, saying in a solemn voice, 'Highness, kiss the Redeemer and Savior of your son. You will see him again after long years, this son of yours who is the object of your deep sorrows, this son whose name is remembered in the cities as well as in the villages. . . . But before that memorable day there will have occurred many changes in France's government: There will be civil wars, streams of blood will be shed and Europe will be all on fire. But Napoleon the Great will return to exhort France, whereon all the countries of Europe will resent her influence. Consider the great work that Napoleon is destined, by the King of Kings, to accomplish!'

"The stranger who thus spoke appeared as a prophet inspired of God, sent by Him to a mother to announce his inviolable wishes as to the destiny of her son. Madame continued to hear him in a kind of ecstasy, until at last he withdrew to leave her to her profound reflections.

"This singular visit, said M. Colonna, seemed to have brought back hope to Madame's spirits, to the point where she had made for the people of the household entirely new liveries. Hope continued to animate her until the second priest of St. Helena—the Abbé Vignali—came to tell her that on the very same day and about the hour when the stranger had been presented to her in Rome, the Emperor had died in St. Helena.

" 'Her Highness,' added Mme. de Sartrouville, 'has told me more than once of that strange visit.' M. Colonna said only that the stranger had the Emperor's tone of voice, his appearance and expression, his impressive manner, his form and figure and walk; that he so resembled him as to be mistaken for him.

"All the searchings throughout Rome and its environs to find the stranger were useless—he had disappeared like a shadow, without leaving the slightest trace" (Barron Larrey, *Madame Mère*, edition of 1892, Vol. II, pp. 248 *ff.*).

That is all that is recorded of this strange affair. That these very reputable people believed they had had this unaccountable experience is beyond doubt. If one must have a practical and factual explanation, then it is best supplied by the Robeaud thesis and the fact that even then Napoleon was living in Verona, had been apprised of the impending death of his double on St. Helena, and, strangely disturbed, had gone to visit his mother in Rome. The

WHO LIES HERE?

day and hour of his arrival would be pure coincidence, of course —and some of his reported speech might be due to the emotional disturbance occasioned in his auditor. If this falls short of explanation, there is nothing else to do but put down the whole circumstantial and evidential account as fantasy.

Epilogue

The worship of God is honoring his gifts in other men, each according to his genius, and loving the greatest men best. Those who envy or calumniate great men dishonor God—for there is no other God.

—Blake

S OME FEW years ago considerable public interest was created by reports that a lock of Napoleon's hair had, under a new technique of chemical analysis, evidenced a high content of arsenic. That this interest is still current is illustrated by the fact that almost any book written on Napoleon since that time gives some attention to the matter, and people who can recall little else of Napoleon's life will inform you gravely that he was without doubt poisoned.

Were a charge of murder against someone yet living being investigated, several pertinent questions would have to be answered before so serious a charge could be maintained. First it would be necessary to prove that the lock of hair was indeed derived from the scalp of the murdered party, and then the exact date of its removal would be needed. In regard to locks of hair purporting to be Napoleon's (and there are several known to be in existence, since it was a sentimental habit of people in the eighteenth and nineteenth centuries to give such mementoes to friends and relatives, as a symbol of regard), these vital questions ought by all means to be answered.

It is recounted—and, I believe, reliably so—that Napoleon gave locks of his hair in 1818 both to Betsy Balcombe and to Captain Poppleton, a British orderly officer who had carried out his duties so pleasantly that the Emperor wished to give him some testimonial of his regard. Hair obtained at this period (1818), if found to be charged with arsenic, would tell an entirely different story than hair taken at the time of the decease in 1821. Arsenic found in the earlier sample, when Napoleon showed no signs of ill health, could reasonably be assumed to have been a lifetime's incidental assimilation from foods, water or medicines. If found at the later date but not at the earlier one, then the darkest suspicions might be entertained as to its origin—yet even then, not certainly so. Antommarchi dosed his patient with the most unsuitable and violent drugs, among which was tartar emetic in strong drafts: this, a salt of antimony, is found naturally in association with arsenic salts and would not in that age be sufficiently well refined to assure removal of the arsenic.

The consensus of modern physiologists is that the presence of arsenic in these samples is not a proof of any deliberate attempt at poisoning. There is an arbitrary agreement in medico-legal opinion that ten parts per million of arsenic in human tissues can be classed as a normal accumulation—from ingestion of seafood, water and vegetables from arsenic-infiltrated earth, from medicines and so on—and for this amount, at least, there is good tolerance. The arsenic concentration in the hair sample was 10.38 parts per million, sufficiently close to the "normal" limit of 10 parts per million.

There is, of course, a strong temptation to leap to the conclusion of deliberate poisoning, because of the unique situation in which the prisoner was placed. First to be suspected would be the British custodians, who were expending sums variously given as one-half to a full million pounds per annum in guarding and supplying the exiles. Poison could be introduced via the gardeners, perhaps, to a cooperative French chef's assistant within. Montholon has been mentioned as the most likely author of such a deed on the part of

EPILOGUE

the French, since he knew he was to benefit from his master's death by two million francs. Somehow he doesn't seem that base or desperate a man. A better choice, in my opinion, would have been the opportunist Antommarchi—a man of little moral scruple or loyalty.

Certain it is that everyone in Longwood was bored in the extreme: Life passing them by, their confreres at home all pursuing their careers, enjoying the amusements of cities—while there they abode, hopelessly frustrated, waiting for one man to expire and liberate them all. Yes, the atmosphere for a murder, for an assist to stubborn nature, was certainly present. But despite all that and the arsenical hair, there isn't enough evidence; death had a sufficient *entrée* already established and needed no goading. The strong aura of suspicion that exists about the death of Cipriani in 1818 may play a part in predisposing the mind toward a consideration of a similar crime in 1821—but the two instances are far from parallel. Dr. R. Turner's review of this matter speaks for the attitude of most modern pathologists. (His well-reasoned article is quoted in Martineau's *Napoleon's St. Helena.*)

But if this man who died on St. Helena in May of 1821 was indeed the onetime *voltigeur* Robeaud, double of the Emperor Napoleon—what then was the subsequent career of Napoleon, after his escape in 1818?

At least one thing is certain—that for three years he remained obscure, inactive, until the news of the death on St. Helena set him free. Had he taken part in any military adventure during that period, his name would doubtless have become known through his prowess, and a terrible calamity would have befallen his friends of Longwood: participants all, or almost all, in the plot that had given him his liberty. He himself, of course, would have received

WHO LIES HERE?

short shrift had his identity been suspected in Europe—or in almost any part of the world accessible to his political enemies.

The part of the legend introducing "Revard" and "Petrucci" and Verona and Schönbrunn has at first a rather too apt appearance, as of something contrived, perhaps . . . and yet, why out of all the world's cities was Verona selected? And that unusual occupation of diamond merchant (since some sort of an involvement with business seemed desirable as a further shield against public curiosity) was really an appropriate and useful one for a man who had habitually kept much of his wealth in gems. Verona, also, aside from its happy associations, was not too remote from the place where his son was held a perpetual prisoner of the Austrian Emperor. Finally, nothing is more likely than Napoleon, bored by years of inactivity, racing northward on learning of the serious illness of his loved boy—there to make rendezvous with the bullet that had missed him on so many battlefields.

In spite of all that, however, there remain fragments that appear less conceivable—the unlikely concern, for example, of the alienated and adulterous Marie Louise to have the slain intruder buried in her "private plot" at Schönbrunn; the Austrian imperial family are interred, all one hundred and thirty-eight of them, each in a leaden casket in the imperial crypt of the Kapuzinerkirche. The remains of Marie Louise herself lie there amidst the grim throng, a posy of artificial violets on her sarcophagus providing a pathetic dot of color in the prevailing grayness. The space once occupied by her son—hers and Napoleon's—is now vacant; the casket of the Duke of Reichstadt was sent to Paris by Hitler as a placatory gesture, a vain attempt to create goodwill for the Nazi regime among the collaborators. Today it lies under the Invalides dome, close beside that of the man assumed to have been his imperial father.

The Schönbrunn garden story could then have been the true

EPILOGUE

one—it is reputed to have taken place only two years after Robeaud's death, which leaves but little time to be accounted for. Those years could very well have been spent, as Napoleon had so often expressed the wish of spending his last years, in anonymity and well-earned rest. It may be doubted that he had any considerable time left to him, after so furious a combustion as his life represented; his determination to escape St. Helena could be interpreted as a duty he owed to his own conception of his stature and integrity—the need to die a free man and not the humbled prisoner of a people whom he felt had so grossly insulted and betrayed him. Moreover, he may have wished to prove to himself—and perhaps to those who came after—that even though his genius and energies might no longer have been at their pristine peak, he could yet think his way out of the tightest prison the world had been able to devise for him.

If his career was to take him to an end other than the legendary one of Schönbrunn, if the call to arms still clamored in his blood—the place to seek for signs of his presence would be in South America, where great struggles for freedom from Spain were taking place, and many a soldier exiled from Europe was making a warrior's name for himself. There are, indeed, tales of this sort extant, but none that carries much flavor of conviction. It remains but a speculation that Napoleon served in either South America or in Mexico as a *Liberador*. But of this we can be most certain: Had he wished to lead an army in such a cause, he would have been made very welcome indeed!

It might seem that there should be more signs of his onetime residence in Verona, a record of his passing in the official records of Schönbrunn. There are printed references to the story of Petrucci and Revard to be found in Veronese books of curiosa—always as part of a legend, however, and not as history. As for the city, it bears little resemblance to that of Napoleon's day, and no fortune

WHO LIES HERE?

would attend any effort to rediscover the ancient address of the diamond merchant—even if one knew what it had been. At the University of Verona there are some who know of the story, even though no one has attempted a search of the old newspaper files or civic records. The conclusion of those knowledgeable in the matter, one finds, is that the legend has had considerable local currency, with revivals of interest from time to time, but that it is unsupported by any available documentation.

In Schönbrunn the researcher will encounter another brick wall, with some reinforcement added over and above that of Verona. Here, in addition to a certain official reluctance to admit to anything, no matter in what connection, that might appear to contain in itself elements of historical irregularity or possible national denigration, there exists a well-recognized condition of confusion in the National Archives owing to the disruption and destruction of the last war. A professional researcher whom I later attempted to enlist in my endeavor provided the information that the Viennese custodians are in some despair over the condition of their historical records, and that as a result they quite often refrain from entering into any embarrassing correspondence concerning them. The destruction or loss of old documents and letters during and after the war was so great that in some instances only a few items remain of once vast collections.

The impression given is that neither northern Italy nor Vienna will represent, for years to come, anything approaching a happy hunting ground for the researcher in historical documents. And that is the world's loss.

The trail, in brief, seems to be lost here. Perhaps this is because it was intended that it should be. The ex-Emperor may have fully realized that his public career was over and that from then on and for the remainder of his life he must shun all involvements that might bring him to the public eye—thus avoiding the assassins,

EPILOGUE

kidnappers and extortionists that otherwise would surely be baying on his trail. He may also have lost the enthusiasm for a return to his old *métier*—war and command and the machinations of diplomats and financiers. A peaceful enjoyment of life as a private citizen, secure in his moderate degree of wealth, may well have seemed the *summum bonum* to his jaded spirit.

But if the end escapes the researcher, what of the earlier part of the legend, that of Robeaud and Baleicourt?

The chief difficulty here is finding the place! So truly obscure is this tiny hamlet that even French consuls will own themselves beaten—but not the Michelin people: their map Number 57 locates it properly as being about 247 kilometers from Paris and about six kilometers to the west of Verdun. The hamlet next to it is named, prophetically, *Regret*.

From the Gare de l'Est in Paris the train passes through a succession of names rendered famous in the first world war —Meaux, Chateau Thierry, Epernay . . . names memorable to a generation still living as sites of stubborn resistance and monstrous assaults that reduce the statistics of Napoleonic struggles in the same country to almost contemptible proportions. And so forward, passing through the Champagne country to change trains at Chalons-sur-Marne and turning more northward to approach even grimmer Verdun. In the Emperor's time Verdun had an unsavory reputation for many an English sailor and soldier imprisoned there, as well as in the memories of the English colony interned after the rupture of the Peace of Amiens in 1802. But it attained its full grandeur—a somber and oppressive one that still seems to hang over the city—in the fierce and murderous defense of 1916-17 and in the fury of the final successful counterattack.

In the well-appointed *Bibliothèque Municipale,* standing in the lee of the shell-scarred twelfth-century cathedral, can be found the carefully printed and bound annals of the city and its surrounding

WHO LIES HERE?

townships—yes, those of Baleicourt included. That Baleicourt should yet stand and that its ancient records should be available and so admirably preserved seems matter for marvel. Throughout the breadth of this stern country the questing traveler may too often come upon the little white sign that declares, simply and eloquently: "Here stood the village of ———, destroyed in 1917"—or in some adjacent year. Poor Baleicourt! It seems that even the colossal artillery barrages must have passed over it, the locked armies, in search of worthier targets, shunning it by mutual indifference. It would seem that the passage of centuries has barely registered on it, it appears so securely tied into the very earth itself—a humble collection of barns and huts whose outlines emerge from the soil to continue its contour briefly and somberly, leaving no recall of its presence in the observer's mind. It is impossible to find a picture postcard of the place, even in Verdun: It has as successfully repelled all cameramen as it had the arms and armies of the world.

And yet someone, or rather several people, took the trouble to record for perpetuity the vital statistics of the hamlet created through the centuries; alack, among them there is no name of Robeaud written down, neither in the year 1781 nor in any other of twenty or more years before or after it! Nor is there a Robeaud in any other village in the community of Verdun—nor, so scanty the local populations, in the past at least, is there even an "R" category!

No Robeaud? What price then the account of that intriguing obliterated date of his demise—that *"died in St. Helena on* ———"?

Well, there *is* a pamphlet; it is entitled *The Napoleon of Baleicourt,* for the legend has been here first, as elsewhere. Here it is narrated well and at some length, for it is more replete with detail and circumstance than any other version one may come upon. The remarkable thing about it is that the writer appeared to

EPILOGUE

have resented the notoriety thus afforded Baleicourt, to have
harbored a wish to suppress it. He sums up the case in this manner:

> There are here, most certainly, enough reports of docu-
> ments, facts and dates! If they were confirmed, this
> thesis would at once take on a very serious aspect,
> worthy of attentive consideration. We ourselves have
> had sufficient curiosity to wish to verify these dates,
> facts, and documents of our Verdun region; we have set
> on foot researches in the old registers of the civil gov-
> ernment in storage at the town hall of Verdun
> —Baleicourt being a dependency of this city. We have
> carefully gone through the records of the Parish of St.
> Amant—to which pertained, around 1780, the sei-
> gneury of Baleicourt—with regard to the births and
> deaths that occurred in this hamlet. However, we have
> searched in vain for the birth of Robeaud on the date of
> July 19, 1781—or on any date near it. In fact we have
> not found the name Robeaud, under births, marriages
> or deaths, in any year up to 1832.

To this declaration the name of V. Schleiter is appended, with the
date of December, 1932.

It is true that the handwritten originals of the vital records are
still stored at the town hall, even as they appear to have been in V.
Schleiter's time. It was impossible then to find out anything about
him, save that he was not a known historian—but about halfway
down the Rue Garibaldi there is a little memorial park and its
marble plaque set amid the shrubbery. It bears a relief portrait of a
gentleman impressively moustached, and the bronze letters beneath announce that this is V. Schleiter himself—Mayor of Verdun and Deputy of the Meuse. His death had taken place, appar-

WHO LIES HERE?

ently, in the year following that in which he had composed his little monograph defending the integrity of his township against loose historical attributions.

Alas for fame—alas for civic distinctions!

No wonder he had employed the editorial "we," that he had exhibited such ready access to the stored records of the town hall! One need hardly dog the footsteps of such a man, nor presume to review his findings—his word alone will suffice since there are also those creditably reproduced facsimiles at the Municipal Library.

No Robeaud!

That Verona and Vienna should alike prove frustrating is to be expected, since in both these places official secrecy might well have precluded any permanent recording of events of such appalling implications. One would need to be a researcher of enormous skill and persistence and wealth—preferably a resident of many years in either place or both—in order to be fortunate enough to come upon such a reference as that, for example, in the private diary of the *"Procureur Karl Arnstein, en fonction"* at Schönbrunn that tragic night of September 5, 1823.

But as Mayor Schleiter so firmly shows, there was never a Robeaud born, married, or buried in or around Verdun in any year in the least to be implicated in the facts of the legend.

But there *was* a Robeaud. His vital dates are known, his regiment and the name of his colonel, the officer who discovered him. The chief of Napoleon's police, Fouché, received him and the police agent LeDru records him—and beyond all that we have seen and considered the cumulative evidence of his three years on St. Helena and his demise there.

There must have been—there has been—deliberate misdirection here. That, when one stops to consider it, was to be expected. Because of it, must one feel obliged to discard and forget all that

EPILOGUE

astonishing list of facts one has come upon, the long series of events not in the least explicable without the "Robeaud" thesis, culminating in the physical impossibility of reconciling the characteristics of that man autopsied on May 6, 1821, with those of the Emperor Napoleon? Not one of these important facts can be disputed, nor ought they to be shrugged away or regarded with indifference. There was—it is necessary that there was—a Robeaud. What does it matter what it was finally agreed on to name him?

Why Baleicourt was selected as his birthplace one cannot possibly guess, unless there was a need to find for that purpose the most humble, most obscure or even wretched of all the hamlets of France. Otherwise it must have been named by blind chance; possibly the name of the town has become corrupted over the years, or it may have been deliberately disguised from the first—it could, perhaps, have derived from some other name ending in -*court*. But if one were determined to search through the civic records of every such possible village, a lifetime would barely suffice!

This much can be conceived: That whether his name or the name of his town be disguised or not, a man whom we may continue to call Robeaud was taken to St. Helena in 1818 and the Emperor Napoleon taken away—in some such manner as this book indicates. Otherwise there is no value in circumstantial evidence.

One may be glad, moreover—in spite of all the thwartings —that the search for Robeaud ends in defeat and frustration. The renown of the Emperor will ever flourish, serene in the austere magnificence of Les Invalides, his legend fixed permanently in the hearts of men who revere genius and energy: This is what he wished for and arranged and planned for. Yet if the occupant of that splendid tomb be but a humble private soldier, that too would have been by the Emperor's design and will—a part of his little

WHO LIES HERE?

joke on a people who so coldly repudiated him at the last; on those arrogant ones also, across the narrow seas, who, profiting by his momentary indecision, had had the audacity to conceive of the great Napoleon as "done for"!

No matter where a great one rests his spirit is and ever will be universally present.